LEADING YOUR INSURANCE AGENCY TO GREATNESS

Based on:

The Five Tiers Of Agency Leadership

DICK BIGGS
& SCOTT FOSTER

All Scripture verses are from the Open Bible, New Living Translation (NLT).

ISBN: 1499727755
ISBN 13: 9781499727753
Library of Congress Control Number: 2014910144
CreateSpace Independent Publishing Platform
North Charleston, South Carolina

TABLE OF CONTENTS

DEDICATION

We salute the nearly fifty agents and other leaders who contributed their time and tremendous thoughts to this undertaking. You'll find their pearls of wisdom sprinkled throughout these pages. If we listed all of their impressive accomplishments, it would take another book. So in the interest of brevity, you'll find only their names, titles and locations listed below.

A couple of contributors chose anonymity and we've honored their request. We appreciate all of you—named and unnamed—for making the time to share your insights and experiences. What's especially refreshing is that in today's politically correct environment, so many agents gave thanks to God for being blessed with such a splendid entrepreneurial opportunity. We're eternally indebted to these contributors:

Christine Bailey, Agent, Moss Bluff, LA
Kirk Baker, Agent, Valencia, CA
Brooks Baltich, Agent, Richmond, VA
Sully Blair, Agent, Bennettsville, SC
Gale Breed Jr., Agent, Lincoln, NE
Terri Brock, Agent, Columbia, SC
Shannon Brooks, Agent, Amarillo, TX
Art Brucks, Agent, Burleson, TX
Steve Cannon, Agent, Woodstock, GA
Dave Christy, Agent, Spokane, WA (three locations)
Al Clark, Agent, Arlington, TX
Dan Combs, Agent, Dalton, GA
Ray Cornprobst, Retired Field Leader, The Villages, FL
Jim Cornwell, Agent, Tampa, FL
Tom Davis, Agent, Oxford, MS
Chris Dorris, Agent, Hoover, AL

Bill Epperly, Retired Field Leader, Chicago, IL
Sam Eubank, Field Leader, Newburgh, NY
Scott Garvey, Agent, Baltimore, MD
David Haymon, Agent, Leesville, LA
Pat Healey, Agent, Lake Oswego, OR
Denis Husers, Retired Field Leader, Lake Charles, LA
Todd Jackson, Agent, Anchorage, AK
P. J. Johnson, Agent, North Charleston, SC
Johanna Kelly, Field Leader, Binghamton, NY
Mark King, Financial Services Rep, Conyers, GA
Bill Kolb, Agent, Pryor, OK
Tommy McQueeney, Agent, Charleston, SC
Greg Monroe, Field Leader, Greenville, NC
Dave Munson, Agent, Ellicott City, MD
Doug Nichols, Agent, Knoxville, TN
Phil Nichols, Agent, Knoxville, TN
Perry Olson, Agent, Las Vegas & Henderson, NV
Cliff Ourso, Agent, Donaldsonville, LA
Terri Phillips, Contact Center Training Manager, Dallas, TX
Tony Pope, Agent, Summerville & Mount Pleasant, SC
Trey Rhodes III, Agent, Newnan & Carrollton, GA
Don Rood Jr., Field Leader, Los Angeles, CA
Matt Schomburg, Agent, Katy, TX
Dan Sevigny, Founder, PayIgniter, Helotes, TX
Stan Simmons, Agent, Lawrenceburg, KY
Bill Thorp, Agent, Grants Pass, OR
Isabelle Waldrep, Agent, Forsyth, GA
E. G. Warren, Agent, Gulfport, MS
Gary Welch, Agent, Peoria, IL
David Wilcox, Agent, Gonzales, LA
Tom Wright, Agent, Porterville, CA

SPECIAL DEDICATION:

The late **Bob Joiner** was a legendary field leader for a major insurance company. He retired in Columbia, South Carolina, was diagnosed with stage IV cancer and passed away about a year later. Bob was a special person, a dedicated family man, a commendable Christian role model and our friend. We know Bob would be proud of this book because he was all about helping agents become better leaders and grow their businesses. We miss you, Bob!

We'd also like to thank **Terri Phillips**, contact center training manager for a major insurance company, for not only contributing some pearls of wisdom to our book but also going the extra mile to provide solid editorial advice. We appreciate you, Terri!

Finally, we're grateful to **Jan Truelove** at Office Pros in Gainesville, Georgia for her special expertise in graphics. You're the best, Jan!

THOUGHTS FROM DICK BIGGS

Scott Foster and I met in 1989 and we've been good friends ever since. Thankfully, Scott invited me to speak to his agency team on October 12, 1990. This one engagement opened the door for me to deliver countless customized leadership programs to hundreds of agents at the insurance company Scott represents. Judy and I are also proud to be multiline customers at Scott's award-winning agency.

This book is Scott's idea. I'd thought about it over the years, but other priorities always seemed more pressing. Now, thanks to Scott's encouragement, we've created a resource that we trust will stimulate your thinking. More importantly, we hope you'll act on what you read.

You'll find this to be more of a big-picture book than a compilation of how-tos. Sure, there are many specific strategies within these pages, but our primary purpose is to help you formulate a long-term view toward agency growth. If you're opposed to expansion, what's holding you back? Don't you have access to the same resources that growing agencies do?

No doubt this book will be read by agents at all levels of experience and production. If you're a relatively new agent, you may feel like you're drinking from a gushing fire hose of information. If you've been an agent for several years, you'll probably be challenged to try some things you may have resisted in the past. If you're a veteran agent, perhaps you'll be reenergized by some of the innovative ideas within these pages.

To maximize the return on your investment of time, please keep an open mind while reading this book. If you have a negative attitude toward learning and growing, perhaps these words will convince you to think more positively. Complete the "call to action" section at the end of each chapter. Consider doing a book study with your team members, agent peers or any others in your learning circle. Get objective feedback. Create an action plan. You'll discover true fulfillment in the quest for agency greatness. Enjoy the journey!

Note: When you see the word "I" on these pages, it's coming from me. When referring to my coauthor, it will say "Scott Foster." The company represented by the contributing agents and other leaders is purposefully unmentioned. In addition, we've intentionally avoided using any proprietary language or acronyms associated with this renowned insurance and financial services organization.

THOUGHTS FROM SCOTT FOSTER

Dick Biggs is more knowledgeable about our business than any other outside speaker I've ever seen. He's familiar with our history. He understands our culture. He speaks our language. And he's very in tune with agency challenges to the point that agents often ask him at seminar breaks, "Now, Dick, where is your agency located?"

I invited Dick to take on this project for two reasons. (1) This material can help you become a better leader. (2) These ideas can help your agency grow and improve. Obviously, there are many ways to operate an agency, including the option to stay right where you are. If that's you, perhaps this message will be timely, uplifting and transformational.

I've been in this profession for more than four decades and, candidly, there's never been a better time to lead your agency to greatness. Why coast on a sea of comfort when you can soar on skies of peak performance? These ideas can help you achieve such a worthy goal, but you must turn reading into results or nothing will change for the better.

I'm dedicated to lifelong learning because it's the difference between agency stagnation and growth. I urge you to expand your agency not for egotistical or monetary reasons, but because it will help you serve your customers more diversely and deeply in the critical areas of insurance and financial services; it will inspire your team members to reach their full potential; and it will enable you to leave a leadership legacy worthy of emulation.

Are you up for the challenge? If so, get ready to participate in an exciting learning opportunity—one that will take you and your team to new heights of professional success and personal satisfaction.

Note: The agents who were interviewed for this book are with the same major insurance company I represent. Many of us offer a wide range of insurance products and financial services. Consequently, this book is targeted at full-service agencies. However, if you're an agent who sells limited products or you don't lead a big team, perhaps our message will persuade you to become a more multifaceted agency.

HOW DO YOU RATE AS AN AGENCY LEADER? (ASSESSMENT)

To assess how you're doing as an agency leader, answer these twenty provocative questions with a *yes* or *no*. Then, check your score to see what you're doing right and how you can improve:

- Do you have a regular time and place set aside to think about your agency? _____
- Do you have a firm commitment to constant leadership development? _____
- Do you consistently remind your team of the agency purpose statement? _____
- Do you consistently remind the team of your bold agency vision? _____
- Do you consistently model the conduct you want your team to emulate? _____
- Do you demonstrate a high level of energy/expectations to your team? _____
- Do your team members know their roles in fulfilling the agency purpose/vision? _____
- Do you challenge your team members to set lofty goals? _____
- Do you offer the right incentives to help team members achieve their goals? _____
- Do you find ways to turn your business plan into a living, breathing document? _____
- Do you encourage your team members to be creative and innovative? _____
- Do you ask team members for their ideas/feedback? _____
- Do you ask questions to help team members learn how to solve their problems? _____

- Do you ask each team member for a progress report at your agency meetings? ____
- Do your team members have a specific program for their ongoing growth? ____
- Do you consistently maintain a high level of team longevity? ____
- Do you conduct an annual agency planning retreat? ____
- Do you actively cultivate strong bonds with your team members? ____
- Do you hold your team accountable for their performance? ____
- Do you take responsibility for your team's underperformance? ____

Scoring: Number of *yes* answers ____ Number of *no* answers ____
17–20 *yes* answers: You're a superb leader. **13–16** *yes* answers: You're on the right path to effective leadership. **9–12** *yes* answers: There's definitely room for improvement as a leader. **8 or fewer** *yes* answers: You have some work to do. Now, please review your *no* answers and create a proactive plan to help you reach your full potential as a leader.

INTRODUCTION

Somehow, "Leading Your Insurance Agency To Mediocrity" or "Leading Your Insurance Agency To Failure" didn't seem like very captivating titles. Instead, we chose "Leading Your Insurance Agency To Greatness." Although leadership mastery has been debated for centuries, you hold in your hands our valiant—and somewhat intimidating—effort to share a collection of thoughts on this ancient deliberation. Therefore, we must ask: What is leadership? What is greatness?

Some people think leadership is innate. Some believe leadership is a learned art. Others feel leadership is a blend of natural ability and dedicated study. Certainly, many people have provided insightful definitions of leadership, including the following gems:

> "Leadership is an invitation to greatness
> that we extend to others."
> –Mark Sanborn, *You Don't Need A Title To Be A Leader*

> "The true measure of leadership is influence—
> nothing more, nothing less."
> –John Maxwell, *The 21 Irrefutable Laws Of Leadership*

> "Leadership is first being, then doing. Everything the
> leader does is a reflection of what he or she is."
> –Warren Bennis, *On Becoming A Leader*

> "Leadership is much more of an art, a belief, a condition
> of the heart, than a set of things to do."
> –Max De Pree, *Leadership Is An Art*

"If there's a clear distinction between the process of managing and the process of leading, it's…managers get other people to do, but leaders get other people to want to do. Leaders do this by first of all being credible…the foundation of all leadership."
–James M. Kouzes & Barry Z. Posner, *The Leadership Challenge*

"Leadership is a potent combination of strategy and character. But if you must be without one, be without strategy."
–General Norman Schwarzkopf

"Leadership is the art of getting someone to do something you want done because he wants to do it."
–President Dwight D. Eisenhower

"Leadership is unlocking people's potential to become better."
–US Senator and NBA Hall Of Famer Bill Bradley

"Management is doing things right; leadership is doing the right things."
–Peter Drucker

"The secret of leadership is simple: Do what you believe in. Paint a picture of the future. Go there. People will follow."
–Seth Godin

Between us, Scott Foster and I have nearly a century of leadership experience. Scott was a National Honor Society qualifier and finished in the top ten of 605 students at Jordan Vocational High School in Columbus, Georgia. He graduated magna cum laude from the University of Georgia with a degree in risk management and insurance. He's a past president of his Kiwanis and Rotary clubs. Scott has chaired several committees at his church, where he has been a Sunday school teacher for twenty-five years. Scott has been a top-ten agent sixteen times, and the top life producer twenty-one times. He helped develop the second phase of a leadership program for the agents of the company he represents.

I was newsletter editor and class graduation speaker at East Atlanta High School in Atlanta, Georgia. As a marine sergeant, I served on the elite security guard duty program at the American embassies in Warsaw, Poland, and Rome, Italy. I'm a former sales manager. I'm a past president of three volunteer organizations. I'm a co-founder of the Chattahoochee Road Runners, the second-largest running club in Georgia. I'm a small group facilitator at my church. I've mentored several agents and other successful professionals. I've been a business owner since 1982.

Here's what we believe about leadership:

Regardless of how someone becomes a leader or how the position is defined, you know a great leader when you see one. I often ask seminar participants to name the qualities they associate with great leaders. What follows isn't meant to be a comprehensive list, but here are the most common **leadership traits** that have been shared over the years:

Accountability, Adaptability, Charisma, Commitment, Common Sense, Compassion, Competence, Congruency, Courage, Creativity, Curiosity, Decisiveness, Dependability, Determination, Focus, Honesty, Humility, Integrity, Passion, Persistence, Persuasiveness, Poise, Positive Attitude, Preparation, Purposefulness, Self-Discipline, Sense Of Humor, Team Player, Vision, Wisdom

This isn't to imply that leaders are perfect. They aren't. This doesn't mean every leader possesses *all* of these qualities. They don't. Yet the bar is set deliberately high for those brave souls who choose to lead rather than follow. While leadership is certainly not a responsibility for the meek, its rewards are more satisfying than most life experiences because of the impact it has on so many people.

You should feel honored to be a leader in the noble profession of insurance and financial services. You make a major difference in the lives of the people you serve every day—team members, customers and others in your community. Your products and services help people minimize their risks and maximize their dreams. Unquestionably, what you do is important.

This brings us to this book's purpose. Paraphrasing Mark Sanborn's definition of leadership, we're extending an invitation to you to pursue greatness, "something remarkable in magnitude, degree or effectiveness...superior in character or quality." What does this look like?

Jim Collins nailed it in *Good To Great*: "Enduring great companies preserve their core values and purpose while their business strategies and operating practices endlessly adapt to a changing world." Specifically, if you want to be a great agency leader, your organization must cherish principles and purpose above profits and production.

If you're a new agent, this book should be especially helpful. If you're a blossoming agent, this book can help you get to the next level. If you're an agent extraordinaire, this book is definitely for you because great leaders are always striving to get better.

Our message comes from a "Mr. Inside & Mr. Outside" perspective. Scott "Mr. Inside" Foster has been an agent with the company he represents since 1976. He's consistently in the top ten out of thousands of agents at this company. I've delivered countless leadership seminars to hundreds of Scott's peers since 1990, hence the "Mr. Outside" moniker. Together, Scott and I are going to share the best of what we've learned on our lengthy journeys.

Speaking of that, my journey received a dramatic boost in 1999 when an insurance executive declared fervently, "Dick, if our agents are going to be fully engaged in offering all of our insurance products and financial services, they're going to have to make the transition from salespeople to small business CEOs." It led to a radical shift from generic trainer to a deliverer of customized leadership material to the agents of a company I've served for nearly twenty-five years.

Fortunately, Gary Lukovich, now retired, was willing to share his broad vision with this speaker at the right time. It was the catalyst for creating *Beyond Agent To Small Business CEO,* which began as a ninety-minute keynote address; evolved into a twenty-module, two-day seminar; and eventually became the twenty-five-chapter book you're now reading. Regardless of how this material has been delivered, the foundation hasn't changed. This is what it's built upon:

The Five Tiers Of Agency Leadership ©

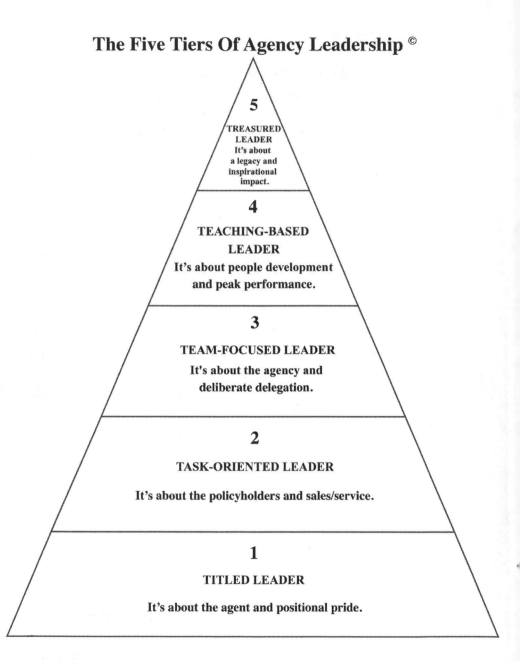

5
TREASURED
LEADER
It's about
a legacy and
inspirational
impact.

4
TEACHING-BASED
LEADER
It's about people development
and peak performance.

3
TEAM-FOCUSED LEADER
It's about the agency and
deliberate delegation.

2
TASK-ORIENTED LEADER
It's about the policyholders and sales/service.

1
TITLED LEADER
It's about the agent and positional pride.

The tiers work like this:

Tier One—The Titled Leader (Ego)

This tier is about *you*, the agent, and *positional pride.* You were given a title upon graduating from agency school—insurance agent—and you should be proud of this memorable achievement. Of course, if you spend the rest of your career patting yourself on the back (ego), you're not going to earn a living or leave much of a legacy. This means you have to get to the next leadership tier as quickly as possible.

Tier Two—The Task-Oriented Leader (Energy)

This tier is about your *customers* and *sales/service.* You have to get busy (energy) doing what will make your agency successful—marketing, prospecting, selling, servicing and so on. It's hard work building a book of business, especially in the early years, but it's also gratifying to know your efforts are helping a lot of people protect their property and lives, prepare for the future, and enjoy priceless peace of mind.

Tier Three—The Team-Focused Leader (Entrustment)

This tier is about the *agency* and *deliberate delegation.* You can't be a do-it-all leader without stressing out or burning out. You must assemble a talented group of associates and rely on them (entrustment) to help you get to your desired destination.

Tier Four—The Teaching-Based Leader (Education)

This tier is about *people development* and *peak performance.* You become a coach, mentor or teacher (education) to your team. The idea is to turn your team members into self-sufficient, peak-performing "mini agents" who reach their full potential under your guidance. This time-consuming, tedious endeavor is often the weakest tier for many agents.

Tier Five—The Treasured Leader (Example)

This tier is about your *legacy* and *inspirational impact.* Frankly, if you excel at the other four tiers long enough, you'll reach this lofty level. It means you're a servant leader (example), an altitude reserved for an elite group of agents who've paid their dues by pouring themselves into the lives of their team members, customers and others in their communities.

You never leave any tier. You simply go beyond positional pride (Tier One) and sales/service (Tier Two) to deliberate delegation (Tier Three) and peak performance (Tier Four) until you make an inspirational impact (Tier Five). It's an intentional game plan that, over time, will enable you, your team and agency to grow beyond your wildest imagination.

Each leadership tier is comprised of five modules for a total of twenty-five modules or chapters. Each chapter features a foundational quote, a theme, three key points and a call to action. If you're already proficient in certain modules, we hope our words will reinforce what you're doing right. If there's room for improvement in certain modules—and we think there will be—keep this in mind: these strategies only work if YOU do!

Whether you're a born agency leader or someone who has to work mightily at your craft, we hope you'll find our ideas refreshing and relevant. In addition, interspersed throughout these pages are pearls of wisdom gleaned from interviewing a host of top producers. We're most grateful to these agents, along with a few field leaders and other executives, for providing such generous contributions to our ambitious undertaking.

Thank you for making time to invest in this material. We urge you to study, discuss and act on what you learn. We're delighted to play a small part in your passionate pursuit toward leadership greatness. God bless you on your pilgrimage.

Scott Foster, Conyers, Georgia
Dick Biggs, Gainesville, Georgia
August, 2014

TIER 1:
THE TITLED LEADER

It's about the agent and positional pride

Loving Leadership

Being Purposeful

Making Difficult Choices

Casting The Vision

Living The Values

Chapter 1:
LOVING LEADERSHIP

"Everything rises and falls on leadership."
–John Maxwell, *Developing The Leader Within You*

Theme:
Are you working more *in* the agency or *on* the agency?

Key Points:
- Making time to think about your agency
- Maximizing performance by minimizing procrastination
- Mastering the art of helping others get what they want

Do you really love your profession? Seriously, do you love leading a team of people who provide vital insurance products and financial services that protect your customers from devastating losses? Or are you merely going through the motions to earn a lucrative living while your thoughts—and perhaps your body—are often elsewhere?

Did you know that your team members and customers can tell if you truly love leadership? You might be able to fake it for a while, but the truth will emerge eventually. If you love leadership, you'll spend ample face time with your team members. If you love leadership, you'll make sure your agency team is big enough and knowledgeable enough to offer all of the available products and services to your customers to minimize their various risks. If you love leadership, you'll encourage others to follow in your worthy footsteps.

There's a big difference between working *in* the agency and working *on* the agency. Back in the day, most insurance agents did the selling, and the secretaries (remember that word?) did most everything else *in* the agency. Today's great agents are focused on leading because they've hired team members to do most of the selling. Consequently, top agents spend the majority of their time working *on* their agencies—casting the vision, creating a bold annual business plan, hiring top talent, training and mentoring team members, holding the team accountable and so on.

P. J. Johnson, an agent in North Charleston, South Carolina, poses this profound question: "Are you the CEO of your business or the best team member? Many agents spend too much time managing the production numbers instead of focusing on the team. In failing to look at the big picture, they end up in the weeds. You have to look toward the horizon, not just the day-to-day activities."

If for some reason you haven't made the transition from salesperson to small business CEO, perhaps you need to take a hard look at why you're procrastinating. In *The 21 Irrefutable Laws Of Leadership*, the first law John Maxwell refers to is the "Law Of The Lid," which says, "Leadership ability determines a person's level of effectiveness." **News flash:** The only person who can put a lid on your leadership potential is you—and only you!

Craig Groeschel, founder and senior pastor of LifeChurch.tv based in Edmond, Oklahoma, suggests you take an honest assessment of the "5Cs": Do you need to boost your *confidence?* Do you need to expand your *connections?* Do you need to improve your *competencies?* Do you need to strengthen your *character?* Do you need to increase your *commitment?* Take whatever steps are necessary to lift that self-imposed lid on your leadership.

Every leader has strengths and weaknesses. If you're not strong in sales and marketing, hire people who are. If you're not strong in organization and business administration, hire people who are. If you're not strong in technology, hire people who are. Your greatest leadership strengths should include delegating, visioning, encouraging, role modeling and mentoring.

Making Time To Think About Your Agency

Don Rood Jr. is a field leader in Los Angeles, California. His primary duty is to help agents grow their businesses within his assigned area. Years ago, we had a stimulating conversation about what it takes to be a fully engaged agency leader. I ended up with a top-ten list, but the first and most memorable point Don shared is this: agents should *make* time to think about their small businesses. (The complete list can be found in chapter 17.)

Agents are often so caught up in the day-to-day necessities of selling products and servicing customers that they fail to think through where they're going and how they plan to get there. Great leaders are prolific thinkers. This doesn't mean you have to spend an inordinate amount of time thinking, because great leaders are prolific doers as well. However, great deeds are usually preceded by some serious thinking and planning.

Have you designated a specific time and place to think about your agency? Whether it's daily, weekly, monthly or less frequently, the important thing is to be an intentional, consistent thinker. Otherwise, the tendency is to be a reactive leader, which often produces unintended consequences. For example, I didn't just sit at my computer and start writing this book. My first priority was to think through the book outline in order to provide clear direction, structure and focus. It was time well spent.

Should it be any different with your agency? Here are some things to reflect on:

- Think about leadership and study it relentlessly.
- Think about what type of leader you want to be.
- Think about your agency vision.
- Think about the talent you'll need to make your vision a reality.
- Think about how you'll gain, train, sustain and retain your dream team.
- Think about the location and physical property of your agency.
- Think about the long-term capital needs of your agency.
- Think about a plan for your personal growth and professional development.
- Think about who you'd like to have as your mentors.
- Think about what kind of leadership legacy you'd like to leave.

David Haymon, an agent in Leesville, Louisiana, takes off every Thursday afternoon to think about his agency. "It's not something you can do well at work because you're immersed in all the daily activities. As a workaholic, it's important to refresh myself, to think about the team and where we want to be, and to make sure I don't burn out. Initially, it was difficult to leave during the week without feeling guilty, but I look forward to it now."

Dan Combs, an agent in Dalton, Georgia, meets regularly with office manager Sarah Gaddis and marketing director Codie Burns to review the agency's purpose, values and goals. Dan says, "We're constantly looking at how we approach our business, and we're not afraid to make changes. We're always open to something new and challenging."

Maximizing Performance By Minimizing Procrastination

We all procrastinate because we're all human. The key is to minimize procrastination by maximizing daily performance. Gary Welch, an agent in Peoria, Illinois, has a terrific slogan: "Make today count!" It's remarkable how quickly days become weeks, weeks become months, months become years and before you know it, you're wondering where the time went.

You and your team can "make today count" by asking the following questions:

- Are we *totally* committed to our noble profession?
- Are we focused more on making money or making a difference?
- Are we wasting time on unnecessary activities?
- Are we doing the most productive things possible every single day?
- Are we making a list of our priorities for the next day the night before?
- Are we chipping away daily at our annual goals?
- Are we learning from our mistakes and moving in a positive direction?
- Are we willing to be held accountable for our actions?
- Are we asking these three questions every day?

Each morning, ask, "What will I do today?" This is your list of **priorities**. Assuming you've planned carefully the night before, you'll be ready to hit the ground running in an organized, focused manner. This simple, effective system will increase your daily productivity.

Beware: If more pressing priorities arise during the day—and they will—do what's most important at that time and then return to your original list of priorities as soon as possible. Remember: a priority is "something meriting attention before competing alternatives."

At the **end of the day**, first ask, "What have I done today?" This is your **performance**. Celebrate what you accomplished. If you didn't achieve all of your priorities, move them to another day until they're completed, or acknowledge that they're no longer important and remove them from your list. Then ask, "What will I keep doing tomorrow?" This is all about **persistence**. If something is working successfully, keep doing it. If not, replace it with a productive activity.

Mastering The Art Of Helping Others Get What They Want

The late orator Zig Ziglar was fond of saying, "You can get everything in life you want if you'll just help enough other people get what they want." That's not a bad definition of leadership. **Fact:** No one achieves *true* success without helping others.

Scott Foster has mastered the concept of helping others get what they want. Scott made it possible for me to speak throughout the insurance company he represents. It was Scott's idea for us to do joint seminars in the areas of agency operations/financial services (Scott) and agency leadership (me). This book was Scott's idea. He loves helping others because he's a giver, not a taker. If there were a list of all the agents Scott has helped during his career, it would be lengthy one.

Key thought: The foremost responsibility of a leader is to discover, encourage and mentor other leaders. If you've accepted this challenge, congratulations! If not, you're missing out on the most satisfying part of leadership. Are you content with the status quo at your agency? Or are you proactively seeking ways to stretch and grow your agency?

Leadership is a special calling, one you shouldn't take lightly, because of the impact it has on so many people. Leadership is an imperfect art, one you should study seriously, craft continuously, practice persistently and teach tenaciously to aspiring leaders. Most of all, leadership is a solemn privilege, one you should accept with humility and gratefulness.

Great leaders respond respectfully to this special calling. Great leaders depend dutifully on this imperfect art. Great leaders embrace eagerly this solemn privilege. How are you doing?

Most people would rather follow than lead, which puts you in elite company. It also means you have to reject or accept the responsibilities of the position. You could remain in a comfort zone and never fully develop your leadership skills. Better yet, you could step out in faith, become a legendary small business leader and reap bountiful benefits reserved only for the intrepid.

Phil Nichols, an agent in Knoxville, Tennessee, and a consistent top-ten producer for the company he represents, says: "I was an average student at Auburn University, where I played football. What I have is street smarts. I'm a good listener. I have a passion for helping people. I've surrounded myself with some quality people, and I love helping them grow. At the end of the day, it's about enjoying what you do. My passion is helping people."

Dan Combs, another top-ten agent in Dalton, Georgia, states: "The reason for our existence is to help others get what they want. I tell my team members that I'm going to pour myself into your success. I'm actively moving team members into leadership positions and giving them opportunities to learn. It's not just about the money; it's about a career path. We're not going anywhere as an agency if the focus is on me."

Denis Husers, a retired field leader in Lake Charles, Louisiana, says: "Thriving agents love leading their teams, hiring new people, and helping them grow. Because they have generous hearts and spirits, they're always looking out for the long-term interests of their team members. This often means helping some team members become agents and be all that they can be."

Here are some proven ways to help your **team members** get more of what they want:

- Show constant appreciation and recognition.
- Encourage through positive feedback.
- Treat everyone with respect and dignity.
- Have caring teaching moments when mistakes are made.
- Ask, "How can I help you?"
- Reward appropriately for peak performance.
- Provide opportunities for ongoing growth.
- Don't micromanage; it destroys confidence and initiative.
- Celebrate successes in fun, creative ways.
- Be a mentor.

Now, here are some ways to help your **customers** get more of what they want:

- Build rapport by finding common interests.
- Focus on their needs, not yours.
- Ask a lot of open-ended questions.
- Listen intently to the answers.
- Follow up promptly on any promises.

- Go the extra mile with service.
- Send handwritten notes of thanks, encouragement and congratulations.
- Be prompt, prepared and professional for all appointments.
- Overcome excuses with education and empathy.
- Position yourself as a valuable resource, not a garden-variety commodity.

CALL TO ACTION

What do you need to DO after reading this chapter?

Chapter 2:

BEINGPURPOSEFUL

"Have a purpose in life and, having it, throw such strength of
mind and muscle into your work as God has given you."
–Thomas Carlyle

Theme:
Are you truly passionate about *why* you do what you do?

Key Points:
- Mission or purpose
- Purpose statements
- The on-purpose agency

Jack McDowell was born into an affluent family in California,
but everything changed when his father became ill. The family
had to move to an abandoned farm in northern Minnesota. At
thirteen years young, Jack worked seven days a week on the farm
and attended school periodically. Despite these tough conditions,
Jack studied late at night by reading great books and taking cor-
respondence courses through the University of Minnesota. Even
though Jack attended high school for less than a full year, he graduated with honors.

Jack's mother said to him when he was ten, "Ask God to help you
find the purpose of your life." She believed his most important
life decisions would be his choice of a vocation and wife. His family was so burdened with debt that it had to sell everything but its

land just to subsist for several years. Jack persuaded a local banker to lend him enough money to buy a car and provide $300 in living expenses until he found a job.

Precocious Jack had an idea. He drove to Dallas, Texas, and arranged an interview with H. L. Hunt, the oil tycoon. This wealthy businessman agreed to sponsor Jack for one year, during which he would help the Salvation Army in Jonesboro, Arkansas, with a fund-raising campaign. It launched an incredible career.

Jack conducted more than one hundred capital campaigns, including seventy-eight for the Salvation Army. His average campaign reached 169 percent of its projected goal. He has raised more money for the Salvation Army than anyone in the world.

Obviously, Jack McDowell found his purpose in life—one that has helped thousands of people. After retiring, he endowed the Jack McDowell School For Leadership Development at the Salvation Army's School For Officer Training in Atlanta, Georgia. Commissioned officers not only learn Christian dogma but also acquire leadership skills.

Jack made another wise decision by marrying Peggy, a successful international businesswoman. At a spry eighty-three, Jack has continued to mentor countless people, including Judy and me, for the past twenty years. He's the author of *The Power Of Purpose*, a book his parents would have loved.

Indeed, great agents are on-purpose leaders. They understand why they do what they do. They can't wait to share their expertise with prospects and existing customers. They know that their efforts matter to people at a time when their needs are the greatest.

Are you as on-purpose as you were when your agency began? If so, I'm guessing you still love why you do what you do. Being passionate about your purpose is contagious. Purposeful team members are more apt to impart such zeal to the customers who make your agency possible. When this happens, your customers are more likely to feel the urgency of buying the important products you provide—and enjoying the subsequent service you render.

If, however, you've lost the passion of your purpose, what happened? Are you frustrated by the changing laws and regulations within your profession? Are you tired of dealing with tough underwriting requirements in your area? Are you facing intense competition and losing customers? Are you struggling with high team turnover? Are you working hard but failing to achieve your goals? Are you falling short as a leader and spending your time elsewhere?

In a speech entitled "How Great Leaders Inspire," Simon Sinek says: "People don't buy what you do; they buy why you do it. And if you talk about what you believe, you'll attract those who believe what you believe." This means you must be able to transfer your head knowledge of your products and services to the hearts of your customers. You can't do that throughout your career if you aren't passionate about your purpose.

Mission Or Purpose

A mission is often comprised of a series of goals, with a specific beginning and end for their accomplishment; for example, think of outer space missions, military missions, diplomatic missions and so on. By contrast, a purpose lasts a lifetime. To know your reason for being, you must ask, "Why am I here?"

Never underestimate the power of purpose, because it defines who you are and what you can become. Purpose is a long-term affirmation of why you do what you do. It gives meaning to your entire life and career. Goals are easier to determine because they're tangible. A purpose is more difficult to develop because it's intangible. The best way to know your life's purpose is to put it in writing.

In an article entitled "Your Greatest Gift," my friend and mentor Jack McDowell asks: "What talent is most responsible for your greatest achievements? It's your *Primary Talent*—and it relates to the purpose for which you were born. I firmly believe each of us was put on this earth for a purpose. Your *Primary Talent* is your greatest gift. There's no finer way to increase the value of your life than to share your *Primary Talent* with those who can benefit from your knowledge and experience."

Hopefully, your *Primary Talent* is leadership—and the reason why you do what you do. Since the purpose of this book is to help you lead your agency to greatness, let's define what this means. It's total dedication to serving your team members, customers and community in a selfless, humble manner. This counterintuitive concept is called servant leadership. After observing such leaders for many years, I can tell you that they have these characteristics:

Sincere—Servant leaders are genuinely concerned about making a difference in the lives of others. They serve out of a sense of duty, not because they're looking for material gain or recognition.

Sacrificial—Servant leaders forgo many short-term pleasures to help others cope with the long-term pain of bad choices, conduct and consequences. In selfless surrender, they're rewarded with true joy.

Sympathetic—Servant leaders have a knack for understanding the plight of others. Perhaps it's because they've also experienced difficult times and someone was there to ease their pain.

Secure—Servant leaders believe in themselves. They know why they're called to help others. They don't think too highly of themselves lest it hinder their altruistic efforts.

Submissive—Servant leaders are humble enough to acknowledge that God created us for a life far greater than self-gratification. They prefer to work behind the scenes and let their actions do the talking.

A Georgia field leader is right on when he says: "We were all created for some specific purpose in life. We're here for a reason. No one else in history has been entrusted with *your* role. You either do your part or the role isn't played. With every passing day, you should see your life's purpose unfolding right before your eyes. Discover and celebrate your genius."

Purpose Statements

Since it's not right to ask you to do something I haven't done, here are the purpose statements for my life and business:

Dick Biggs Personal Purpose Statement: "I will strive to 'to do what is right' by maintaining integrity in all facets of my daily living. I will strive 'to love mercy' by having a positive influence on others as a principle-centered role model and mentor. I will strive 'to walk humbly with…God' through congruency between my beliefs and behavior." (This is based on the guiding principle found in Micah 6:8.)

Biggs Optimal Living Dynamics (BOLD!) Purpose Statement: "Helping organizations boost *bottom line* profits and better the *top line*—people and their productivity."

Now, here are the agency purpose statements of Scott Foster, Cliff Ourso, Dan Combs, Scott Garvey and Chris Dorris:

Scott Foster Agency Purpose Statement, Conyers, Georgia: "Caring, concerned, committed because meeting your needs is our #1 priority."

Cliff Ourso Agency Purpose Statement, Donaldsonville, Louisiana: "We're a team of highly trained professionals who help people discover and understand the financial risks of everyday life. We provide insurance, financial products and services to help people manage these risks, paving the way to reach their financial dreams."

Dan Combs Agency Purpose Statement, Dalton, Georgia: "To meet the expectations of our customers through needs-based selling in a culture that fosters personal growth, peace and happiness while setting a standard of remarkable customer service beyond anyone's expectation—not only by activity, but with productivity."

Scott Garvey Agency Purpose Statement, Baltimore, Maryland: "We energize lives through our performance and passion. We provide confidence and peace of mind to our clients and team members in every interaction."

Chris Dorris Agency Purpose Statement, Hoover, Alabama: "If we don't take care of the customer, someone else will."

Chris adds that his personal purpose statement is "to provide a positive work environment so we can carry out our agency purpose statement." Chris tells his team members that "if you're ever in doubt about anything, please refer to our agency purpose statement."

Steve Cannon, an agent in Woodstock, Georgia, is crystal clear on his purpose: "I look at my agency as a ministry. It's the platform that God has given me. 'Much is required from those to whom much is given' (Luke 12:48, NLT). If a team member or customer is in the hospital, I'm there. If they have deaths in the family, I'm there. I offer to pray for folks and have only been rejected once. I hand out devotional books. When people know my stance, it's amazing how they open up to me."

Steve's agency purpose statement, written when he opened his business on September 1, 1989, is displayed in the lobby and says in part: "From the beginning, the management determined to make God the senior partner. Every day we must reflect the integrity of management, including our senior partner. If sometime we fail on our end, because we are human, we find it imperative to do our utmost to make it right."

If you're unsure about *why* you need an agency purpose statement, here are eight good reasons for creating such a document. An agency purpose statement does the following:

- Demands a sorting out of what's really important
- Requires long-term thinking
- Provides clear direction
- Offers sharper focus
- Builds morale
- Contributes meaning and significance
- Simplifies decision making
- Affords a valuable tool for evaluation and accountability

If you'd like to create an agency purpose statement, but you're not sure how to put your thoughts on paper, the following ten-step formula is a useful guide.

Find a guiding principle as your anchor. You might use a line from a poem, inspirational quote, song lyric, Bible verse or anything else to set the tone for your agency's purpose. For example, Benjamin Disraeli, a British politician and author, said, "The secret of success is constancy to purpose."

Make a list of the agency's dominant interests. These are the important areas where you and your team spend time. Examples include marketing, selling, product knowledge, agent development, team development, finances, community involvement and so on.

List your strongest qualities. Examples include integrity, honesty, reliability, compassion and more.

State your agency's strongest qualities. If some of these qualities are the same as your personal ones, that's OK. It simply means these character traits should probably be a part of your statement.

Jot down some key phrases you feel should be a part of this document. Sample phrases include providing superior service, offering quality products, serving the community, making a difference and so on.

Make an outline. This will save you time and improve the clarity of your statement.

Prepare a rough draft. It's time to incorporate your ideas from the previous six steps into a preliminary purpose statement. Don't be concerned with spelling, grammar or word length. Just get your thoughts on paper for what could be your most important agency document.

Edit, rewrite and polish. Crystallize your thinking. Chop your words. Create a masterpiece.

Ask for feedback from your team and trusted friends. What do they like about it? How can it be improved? Integrate any changes until you're satisfied with the final version.

Put the finished document in prominent places and refer to it often. Read it regularly lest it be filed and forgotten. You might memorize these words over time, but the idea is to live your purpose with all the gusto you can muster.

The On-Purpose Agency

Doug Nichols, an agent in Knoxville, Tennessee, has an interesting approach to being an on-purpose agency. "When I speak to other agents, I always talk about the *why* more than the what. As the leader, you have to set the tone, lead by example and be passionate about why you do what you do. I'm constantly reminding the team of our agency purpose."

Doug refers to a sermon once delivered by Dr. Ronald Stewart, a pastor in Knoxville. It was entitled "The View From The Top." Dr. Stewart said the nearby Great Smoky Mountain National Park attracts twelve million visitors a year—more than any other national park in America.

"For 95 percent of these people," Doug says, "their view is the shops, restaurants, hotels and traffic in towns like Pigeon Forge, Sevierville and Gatlinburg. Only 5 percent of these tourists hike the more than eight hundred miles of trails in the park. Their view is quite different. They see the birds, flowers, trees, beautiful clouds and majestic mountains that seem to go on forever."

Doug's point: "Your view is determined by your purpose. You can go through the motions without thinking about the why. Or you can be on-purpose and get a totally different view of why you do what you do. It's all in how you approach things. I try to avoid negative thinkers, maintain a positive outlook and stay focused on the big picture. To get this view, you have to be willing to pay the price. Are you down in the valley or up on the mountain top?"

Gary Welch, an agent in Peoria, Illinois, is also passionate about purpose. "Most agents and team members are strong at what they do and how they do it, but many don't do well in explaining the why. I'm a crusader for the why. What and how make you success-ful, but understanding the why of our business makes you happy. It's definitely the most important leg of a three-legged stool."

Before becoming an agent, Gary was a field leader for more than three decades. "I'd often ask prospective agents to write a letter saying why they wanted to pursue such a career. Most said they wanted to help people. If they became agents and drifted gradu-ally into a state of complacency, I'd ask them to pull out their 'why I want to become an agent' letter and read it aloud. In many cases, they were surprised by what they'd written years ago."

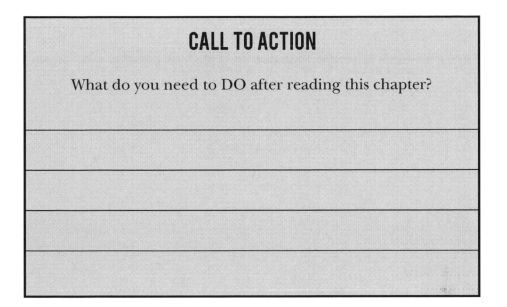

CALL TO ACTION

What do you need to DO after reading this chapter?

Chapter 3:
MAKING DIFFICULT CHOICES

"The difficulty in life is the choice."
–George Moore, *The Bending Of The Bough*

Theme:
Will you summon the courage to be a bold decision-maker?

Key Points:
- Soaring vs. coasting
- Assessing risk vs. reward
- Examining fear vs. faith

The story is told of a woman who was hired to work at an orange-packing plant in California. Her job was to stand next to a huge conveyor belt, pick out any bad oranges and discard them. She quit two days later. When the boss asked the reason for her abrupt departure, she replied, "Sir, I just can't take it anymore. All day long it's decisions, decisions!"

Choosing can be agonizing, but all great leaders are decisive. Decisions determine your direction and desired destination. If you choose to go north on I-85 in Georgia, you won't end up in Alabama. This route will take you to South Carolina and points beyond. Only a fool would head toward a certain destination without first deciding how to get there.

Should it be any different with your agency? If you've made the difficult choices to grow your business, that's a big part of what leadership is about. If you're struggling with the choices you know are necessary for you and your team to soar, take courage because many agents have blazed this path before. You're embarking on a doable undertaking, but you have to move beyond doubt and deliberation to decisiveness and deeds.

Perhaps the toughest choice you'll ever make at your agency is this: Do you want to be the CEO of your small business, develop a team of peak-performing specialists and be perceived as an insurance and financial services resource? Or do you want to operate with a small team, offer limited products and services to your customers and perhaps be viewed as a commodity?

While neither decision is right or wrong, your choice will determine the destiny and legacy of your agency. Have you given serious thought to what your destiny and legacy will be?

Soaring Vs. Coasting

Agents often say to me, "Dick, why should I grow my agency? I'm already making a lucrative income and don't see any reason to expand." Obviously, this is a decision only you can make. Will you settle for mediocrity and perhaps be regretful later? Or will you expand your horizons and strive for greatness? Here are three important considerations to ponder:

First, surplus revenue is a blessing. If you've ever had an agency cash-flow problem, you know how stressful this can be. You're up late at night wondering how or if you'll survive—much less thrive. Steady cash flow provides options that seem like fantasy when times are tough. You can always donate any extra income to a worthy cause, educate your children and grandchildren, save more money for emergencies and retirement, build a new facility, hire more team members and, well, the list is endless.

Second, you'll grow as a leader if you choose to expand your agency. Yes, growth comes with certain risks, but remaining in a comfort zone is also perilous. You could lose customers to more intrepid agents. You'll miss out on hiring potential team members who could take your agency to new heights of fulfillment. Most of all, you won't reach your full leadership potential. Why not dare to be a great leader by making a difference in the lives of as many people as possible?

Third, if you have a smaller team, it's more difficult to have the hard conversations with your customers about *all* of their potential risks. As you know, most customers are required by law to insure their automobiles and homes. But have you talked to your customers about their other needs? What about life, disability and long-term care insurance? What about mutual funds, IRAs, annuities and other investments? What about their banking services?

Stan Simmons, an agent in Lawrenceburg, Kentucky, says: "You've got to be intentional about your business. Lots of agents coast, not because they lack ability but because they're unintentional. Any dead fish can float downstream. You have to be willing to stretch. While it can be painful, it's what helps you grow. Take the time to think about soaring and what's possible. You have to cut through the fog of distractions and be able to distinguish between what's urgent now and what's important over a career."

The following list of contrasts can help you determine if you're a traditional agent or an evolving small business CEO. Place a check mark beside the *one* contrast that describes you best:

- More sales minded **vs.** More leadership focused
- More goal oriented (annual business plan) **vs.** More vision-ary (entire career)
- Sell a limited number of products **vs.** Offer a wide variety of products
- Small staff **vs.** Team of specialists
- Do it all **vs.** Delegator
- Satisfied with the status quo **vs.** Challenged by change and growth
- Front-loaded education (minimal products taught in agency school) **vs.** Career student (multiple products learned over a lifetime)
- No/low technology **vs.** High technology
- More reactive salesperson (P&C) **vs.** More proactive marketer (financial services)
- "We've always done it this way." **vs.** "Let's rethink how we do some things."

If most of your check marks are on the left side, you're a tradition-al agent. If most of your check marks are on the right side, you're an evolving small business CEO.

Assessing Risk Vs. Reward

A synonym for leadership should be courage. Accepting leader-ship responsibility is an admirable act of bravery on your part. It takes guts to be the lead dog, but the view is so much better, if you get my drift.

The late Robert C. Goizueta, a former chairman and CEO of the Coca-Cola Co., once said: "Remember, if you take risks, you may still fail. However, if you don't take risks, you will surely fail. More often than not, the greatest risk of all is to do nothing."

Any risk has the potential for reward or regret. Perhaps the greatest deterrent to taking risks is rationalization. You can justify most any inaction to avoid making a tough decision. This five-point decision-making model is recommended:

Give careful consideration to all the facts and options. This is the logical part of decision making. Does it make sense?

Pay attention to your heart, intuition and gut reaction. This is the emotional part of decision making. How does it feel?

Don't second-guess yourself once you make a decision. It's a waste of time. Learn from your mistakes and move on.

Believe you'll probably make more good choices than bad ones over a lifetime. It's called wisdom for a reason. You get wisdom not from experience but from *evaluated* experience.

Anticipate success, but don't be afraid of failure. Always ask, "What will happen if I don't act? What are the possibilities if I do act? If for some reason I don't succeed, what's the worst that can happen, and can I deal with the consequences?"

Dave Christy is an agent with three locations in the Spokane, Washington, area. When he had been an agent for about a year, he had the opportunity to hear Scott Foster speak. At the time, Scott had about fifteen team members and Dave had one. Dave summoned the courage to approach Scott at one of the breaks: "Mr. Foster, do you remember when you hired your second team member?" Dave said Scott was very gracious to offer this advice: "I always try to hire people with different skill sets to offset my weaknesses."

It takes courage to act on advice that you're uncomfortable with, but it's part of being a great leader. Dave hired a second team member, a receptionist, the following week. "I knew it was possible to grow a team because Scott had done it. He enlarged my thinking."

Dave continues: "I was paralyzed by fear, but you can't grow without making some tough decisions. Now, some twenty years later, I realize a lot of my success is due to taking risks. I believe it's a major reason why we've been profitable and enjoyed consistent growth every year. Incidentally, I'm now in a study group with Scott and some other top agents."

Sam Eubank, a field leader in Newburgh, New York, mentions a study that determined what separates top agents from others. "Essentially, success was tied to the size of the team. Many agents believed it was too hard to manage more than three or four people. They were in a comfort zone not because of production goals but due to team size. They just didn't have the skill set to lead a larger group of people, and it has limited their agency growth."

"Nothing encourages entrepreneurial activity more than the freedom to take risks," states John Steele Gordon, author of *An Empire Of Wealth.* "The word 'entrepreneur' comes from the French and literally means 'undertaker' or 'one who undertakes, manages and assumes the risk of a new enterprise.'" In other words, entrepreneurs are risk takers by nature.

Kat Cole, CEO of Cinnabon, says a leader has "to take a courageous first step. If not, what's the alternative? You can remain in your current environment, or you can be so much more. You just have to figure it out, but it all starts with courage."

Isn't it ironic? Many agents are risk reluctant even though their careers are spent talking to customers about risk management. "The biggest enemy of many agents," says Don Rood Jr., a field leader in Los Angeles, California, "is 'good enough.' They get comfortable. Gradually, the love of talking to people about their risks fades and complacency sets in. They lose sight of what it means to be a risk management advocate. This is when a 'good enough' mentality sets in."

Examining Fear Vs. Faith

Fear can be demoralizing and defeating. I remember the first time Platoon 295 marched by the confidence course at Parris Island, South Carolina, during Marine Corps boot camp. This massive maze of obstacles was frightening and intimidating. The course demands strength, speed, agility, endurance and courage. I had the physical ability from my days as a high school athlete, but my mental outlook needed a boost because I'd never faced such a formidable challenge.

My boost came from our drill instructors (DIs), who didn't expect us to do anything they couldn't execute. These gung-ho leaders demonstrated the proper way to conquer the imposing array of walls, ropes, water barriers and more. The confidence of our leaders was contagious—if they could do it, so could we. Of course, when anyone struggled to overcome a particular obstacle, our energetic DIs didn't hesitate to use some hands-on motivation and harsh tongue lashings to let us know that failure wasn't an option.

How are you creating confidence among your team members and helping them overcome their fears? Unlike a marine DI, you can't make your team members do anything, because they can depart at any time. I couldn't leave Parris Island without severe consequences.

What you can do, though, is influence your team with a positive attitude and supreme confidence in solving daily challenges.

Fact: You're either an attitude buster (negative) or an attitude thruster (positive). For example, mull over these contrasts:

- Do you view difficult situations as problems (buster) or opportunities (thruster)?
- Do you radiate self-pity (buster) or self-confidence (thruster)?
- Do you convey pessimism (buster) or optimism (thruster)?
- Do you favor hurtful criticism (buster) or helpful recognition (thruster)?
- Do you dwell more on fear of failure (buster) or anticipation of success (thruster)?

Shannon Brooks, an agent in Amarillo, Texas, says: "You have to be willing to take a leap of faith or you'll be paralyzed by fear. If you have a 'New Year's resolution mentality,' you aren't serious about overcoming your fears and making the tough choices."

"For example," Shannon explains, "if you join a gym in January to get physically fit, the place is packed. If you're still there in February, most people have forgotten their resolutions, failed to show up and lapsed into their previous bad habits. 'I'm going to' doesn't cut it. To be the best, you have to say, 'Damn the torpedoes, full speed ahead.' You conquer your fears with FIDO—forget it, drive on!"

Shannon's FIDO motto is the way toddlers learn to walk. They don't like falling, but what they dislike even more is limited mobility. Children overcome their fear of falling with a short memory and the courage to keep trying until they get it right. Literally, kids fail their way to success by falling a lot, getting back up and not giving up until they take their first steps. If fear is holding you back, perhaps a little childlike faith or FIDO is just what you need to make the tough choices and grow your agency.

E. G. Warren, an agent in Gulfport, Mississippi, offers this advice: "Once we identify our fears—and we all have them—it's important to communicate them to the team. Try to offset your weaknesses by hiring people with different skills than you. For instance, I'm not very good at technology, but I have people who are. When fears are faced collectively—and each team member is focused on his or her unique strengths—the agency becomes stronger."

In working with agents since 1990, here are some of the most common fears I've heard:

- **Fear of failure.** If I don't succeed, it will be humiliating and embarrassing.
- **Fear of the unknown.** I've never been down this path before and it's scary.
- **Fear of self-limitations**. I don't know if I have what it takes to grow my agency.
- **Fear of undercapitalization.** I'm not sure agency growth is affordable.
- **Fear of what if?** I keep thinking about all of the things that could go wrong.
- **Fear of change.** I dislike getting out of my comfort zone and doing something new.
- **Fear of perfection.** I'm not going to do anything unless it's done exactly right.
- **Fear of accountability.** I don't like having to answer to anyone for my actions.

- **Fear of burnout.** I don't want to work so hard that my health suffers.
- **Fear of success.** I might not be able to deal with getting to the next level.

Interestingly, fear or "anxiety caused by approaching danger" is your friend and foe. Fear can protect you from harm, but it can also be the impetus for venturing outside your comfort zone and reaching your full potential. **Tip:** If you don't conquer your fears, they'll conquer you.

Edmund Burke, an eighteenth-century Irish statesman and philosopher, said it this way: "The concessions of the weak are concessions of fear. No passion so effectively robs the mind of all its powers of acting and reasoning as fear."

My favorite definition of faith is found in Hebrews 11:1 (NLT): "What is faith? It is the confident assurance that what we hope for is going to happen. It is the evidence of things that we cannot see." Choose hope and faith, and then have the courage and commitment to make it happen. You just might be astounded by the results.

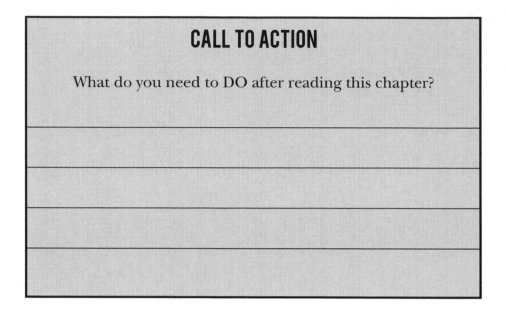

CALL TO ACTION

What do you need to DO after reading this chapter?

Chapter 4:
CASTING THE VISION

"A vision is a mental picture of what could be,
fueled by a passion that it should be."
–Andy Stanley, *Visioneering*

Theme:
What are you working on that's big?

Key Points:
- Goals aren't visions
- The agency vision statement
- Beyond dreaming to doing

After graduating from Dallas Theological Seminary, Andy Stanley received some sound advice from Charles Stanley, his father and a prominent Baptist minister in Atlanta, Georgia. Charles suggested that his son be mentored by a successful businessman. Andy agreed and arranged regular meetings with his mentor.

Andy tells how he dreaded hearing one question almost every week from his mentor: "Andy, what are you working on that's big?" It bothered Andy because he wasn't working on much of anything at the time—and certainly nothing big. In the process, though, Andy was being taught a valuable lesson: great leaders are great visionaries.

There are churches everywhere in Atlanta. Wondering why this metropolis would need another church, Andy decided to start a "church for the un-churched" in an office building in 1995. He wanted to attract people who'd never been to church, people who were returning to church and people who weren't sure what they believed. The concept exploded and the rest is history.

Today, North Point Ministries (NPM) includes five huge church campuses in metro Atlanta, plus more than thirty strategic part-ner churches that follow the NPM model, but are independent of the mother church, at locations across America and around the world. Some twenty-four thousand people attend worship services on a typical Sunday at the five Atlanta campuses. Andy's messages are also heard at the strategic partner churches and on TV and the Internet. His impact has been enormous—and it all started by thinking big.

If you're wondering what this story has to do with your agency, the answer is "everything." How can you expect your team to follow you if they don't know where they're going? As the leader, it's up to you to chart the course for where you're headed in the next five years and beyond. What are you working on—and is it something big?

Goals Aren't Visions

Words have meaning. If I cuss wildly, tell dirty jokes and insult women during one of my presentations, it's unlikely to generate a repeat engagement or any referrals. I might even be removed from the platform—and with good reason—before my program is even finished.

In a similar way, people use certain words all the time and think they mean the same thing. A good example is saying "goal" when you mean "vision" or vice versa. The two words, while related in nature, have different meanings. It's important to understand the distinction.

A goal is a *specific, realistic intention* of what you intend to do daily, weekly, monthly, annually and so on. For example: You want to make thirty calls today. You want to make fifteen sales this week. You want to earn $5,000 this month. You want to be in the top ten agencies in your state this year.

A vision is a *general, idealistic view* of where you'd like to go over the long haul. For instance, when Dr. Martin Luther King Jr. painted a broad picture of racial harmony with his "I Have A Dream" speech in 1963, he was talking about vision. If his speech had been entitled "I Have A Goal," it would have been forgotten long ago because a lot of people have goals.

Dr. King didn't live to see his dream unfold, but his followers developed tangible goals to turn this civil rights leader's vision into a partial and still growing reality. **The point:** Most great accomplishments begin with a dream, vision or big picture "of what could be, fueled by a passion that it should be." Goals are simply the steps needed to make your vision come true.

Vision is a winning combination of imagination and belief. It's imagining something that hasn't happened, yet believing that it has. Do you possess vivid imagination and boundless belief? In *Think And Grow Rich*, Napoleon Hill called it "the power of great dreams." In *Dream Impossible Dreams*, E. J. Ourso said, "Whatever you wish, whatever you dream, whatever you hope to achieve…it's yours if you only believe."

Gale Breed, an agent in Lincoln, Nebraska, agrees: "Everything begins with a vision and deciding where you want to go. You have to find the right team to help you get to your destination. You have to constantly share the agency vision with your team so they can capture your passion. You have to let your team know what your expectations are and set goals to make your vision a reality. It all sounds simple, but it's a lot more difficult to do day in, day out."

Gale continues: "For years, I recruited more out of desperation and struggled due to some poor hiring decisions. I was trying to make things work with the wrong people. I learned the hard way but eventually got people who share my vision. I started with a core of two team members who were competitive and hungry and wanted to be the best. In hindsight, I wish I'd been more systematic with my hiring process."

Andy Stanley says in *Visioneering,* a book with a made-up word and a real message, "Vision weaves four things into the fabric of our daily experience":

Passion—You have to be excited about where you're leading your team members if you want them to share your enthusiasm. A fervent agent tends to have a fervent team.

Motivation—You have to constantly empower your team if you want your vision to unfold. Your inspirational spark or "fire in the belly" is contagious.

Direction—You have to paint the "big picture" of where the agency is headed. Then, create an annual business plan that includes short-term goals for chipping away at the long-term vision.

Purpose—You have to help your team understand *why* they're headed in a certain direction. As the agency leader, it's important to convey this message in a way that fosters total buy-in from the team members you're privileged to influence.

The Agency Vision Statement

An *Atlanta Journal-Constitution* survey produced 50,892 responses to determine the top workplaces in Atlanta. The response receiving the single highest grade (70 percent) was to this question: "Do you believe the organization is going in the right direction?"

CEO Pat Flood of Supreme Lending (Southern Division), which was crowned the premier workplace in the small company category, concurs: "Highly productive employees need a clear vision for where the organization is going and need to understand the plan to get there."

I'm always shocked by how many agents have failed to put their agency vision in writing. Yes, it's a tough thing to do, but it makes the journey a lot clearer. Once it's done, I recommend you post your vision statement in prominent places throughout the agency. There should be no confusion about where you're taking the people who've placed their trust in your leadership.

If you haven't created an agency vision statement, here are some key questions to ask:

- What is my vision?
- Do I truly own my vision?
- Am I really serious about chasing my vision?
- Am I willing to pay the price for following my vision?
- Do I have the right team in place to pursue my vision?

- What strategies are in place to make my vision a reality?
- Will this vision make a positive difference in the lives of my team members, customers and community?

The Scott Foster Agency vision statement, Conyers, Georgia: "To be world famous for exceptional service and sales." This isn't an empty promise. Scott's agency manual supports this vision with the following philosophy:

A Customer is the most important person in this office…in person or by mail. A Customer is not dependent on us…we are dependent on him or her. A Customer is not an interruption of our work…he or she is the purpose of it. We are not doing a favor by serving him or her…he or she is doing us a favor by giving us the opportunity to do so. A Customer is not someone to argue or match wits with. Nobody ever won an argument with a Customer. A Customer is a person who brings us his or her wants. It is our job to handle them profitably to him or her and ourselves.

The Cliff Ourso Agency vision statement, Donaldsonville, Louisiana: "To develop the most highly trained team of professionals by providing them with a continuous stream of strategies, techniques, resources and products for improving their professional and personal lives so they can do the same for our customers."

Note: Cliff's statement is brief and focused on two critical areas— team members and customers. Cliff understands that if he has the right people in the right positions and provides them with a high level of training, they'll be able to do a better job of serving their customers. Cliff is humble enough to realize that if he meets the needs of his team members and customers, his needs will be met many times over. It's called the "Law Of Reciprocity."

In *The 21 Irrefutable Laws Of Leadership*, John Maxwell refers to vision as the "Law Of Navigation," which says, "Anyone can steer a ship, but it takes a leader to chart the course."

Bottom line: Vision is the responsibility of the leader and can't be delegated.

Beyond Dreaming To Doing

While it's important to create an agency vision, the tough part is making it stick. I often get this question at my seminars: "Dick, I cast the agency vision, but we lost sight of it somewhere along the way. Do you have any tips for making my vision last?" Follow these four steps:

State it concisely and clearly. For a vision to take hold, it must be simple, provocative and memorable. It takes a lot of time and effort to crystallize your dream, but brevity and clarity make it a more believable quest.

Cast it convincingly. In order to gain buy-in from your team members, the vision must be conveyed passionately. If you aren't excited about where the agency is headed, why should your team be enthused?

Repeat it constantly. You can't remind the team of your vision too often. Team members love to help you pursue your vision when they understand where they're going, why, and the benefits of making the journey.

Embrace it collectively. No matter how inspiring your vision is, it takes a team to make it happen. When every team member captures the energy of your vision, it creates a synergistic and virtually unstoppable force.

"When I hire new team members," explains Doug Christy, an agent with three locations in the Spokane, Washington, area, "I like to paint the big picture of how they can help us get where we're going. I define the expectations when interviewing prospective team members. I say what needs to happen for them to be successful. I let them know an unsustainable amount of work is not a good job description because it will lead to burnout. Finally, I invite them to come with me on this journey."

Bill Kolb, an agent in Pryor, Oklahoma, states: "I must convey the vision to my team. Otherwise, everything is reactionary. We need to drive the train, particularly in times of upheaval and change. The vision enables us to create a game plan, with every team member playing a role. It's not about me; it's about us. Having a road map makes the journey so much easier and faster. We need to know where we're going. We need to know how we're going to get there. We need to know what will be there when we arrive."

Matt Schomburg, an agent in Katy, Texas, says his vision has changed over the years. "This business is so much bigger than a paycheck. After graduating from Texas A&M, I interviewed with a stock brokerage firm. A manager walked me over to a window, pointed to a fancy car in the parking lot and bragged, 'I want you to work as hard as possible so I can make my payments and keep driving that car.' This didn't seem like a very good way to paint a vision.

"When I started, my vision was to have a bigger agency than my mother, aunt, uncle and grandfather had. [Note: Matt has been a top-ten agent, so that dream has certainly been realized.] As I've

50

matured, my vision has changed. Now, I want to keep growing by being an integral part of our customers' lives as they enjoy what we call the 'Schomburg Experience.' It's our way of taking over our community. Hopefully, I'm doing a good job of casting this vision to my fifteen team members."

Shannon Brooks, an agent in Amarillo, Texas, says this about vision: "The speed of the leader dictates the speed of the team. If you lack passion, you're in the wrong business. You don't have to be the smartest person, but you do need to find good people to help you get where you want to go. Why wouldn't you want to be the best you can be?"

If you doubt the importance of vision, heed this advice from Chris Dorris, an agent in Hoover, Alabama: "You need a one-year vision, a five-year vision, and a ten-year vision. For example, we were among the top fifty agents, then the top twenty-five agents, so we decided to make the top ten in 2013. I put all of Scott Foster's numbers from 2012 up on the board and told my team, 'This is what we need to do to make it happen.' We made it because we envisioned it!"

At a seminar in Ohio several years ago, an insurance company executive was asked to say a few words before my morning program. His opening line, excluding the company name, was this: "There has never been a better time to be an [insurance] agent." The audience laughed heartily. While I loved his comment, it didn't seem like a funny one. Later in the day, I asked an agent about the executive's "humorous" line. "Oh," replied the agent, "Mr. B. has been sharing that optimistic vision with us for years!"

In the pursuit of your agency vision, may these words be a source of encouragement:

Beyond Dreaming To Doing
By Dick Biggs

It's a blessing to dream, a divine dynamic
Is your vision bold, is it panoramic?
A future that's bright if you'll solemnly vow
To follow your heart, to imagine somehow.

Turn dreams into passion, a burning desire
Choose grandiose goals that intrigue and inspire.
A fire in your belly, a gleam in your eye
Motivation so strong that none can deny.

Yet dreams and desires aren't sufficient enough
Decide to act NOW or your road will be rough.
Intentions mean nothing if you hesitate
Why, your life could pass by while you contemplate.

Dare to perform, live up to your potential
For success to unfold, deeds are essential.
If you'll just get busy, there's much you can do
Persevere, my friend, because dreams do come true.

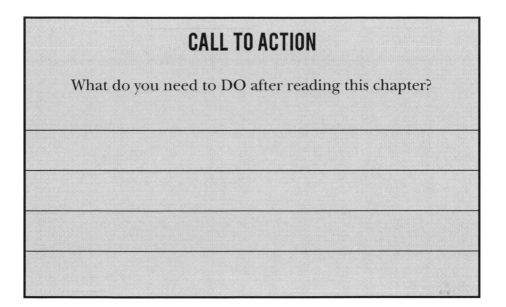

Chapter 5:

LIVING THE VALUES

"Values are the uncompromisable, undebatable
truths that drive and direct our behavior."
–Dr. Ken Boa, *The Perfect Leader*

Theme:
Do you demonstrate daily that character counts?

Key Points:
- Integrity—being true to self
- Honesty—being truthful with others
- Reputation—your character (or lack of it) as seen by others

When I talk about values in my seminars, I have the participating agents do a simple but profound exercise to help them identify what's most important to them. I distribute a sheet of paper containing some of the most common values shared by thousands of people over the years:

Accountability	Fitness/Health	Leadership	Teamwork
Achievement	Freedom	Love	Trust
Appreciation	Friendships	Loyalty	Wealth
Balance	Generosity	Passion	Wisdom
Commitment	Growth	Perspective	_____
Communication	Happiness	Purity	_____
Compassion	Honesty	Recognition	_____
Competence	Honor	Respect	_____
Courage	Hope	Responsibility	_____
Determination	Humility	Service	_____
Discipline	Integrity	Simplicity	_____
Faith In God	Justice	Status	_____
Family	Knowledge	Success	_____

First, I invite the agents to add any other values they feel should be on this list. Second, I ask the agents to circle half of the values, the ones that are most significant to them. This doesn't mean the rest of the values aren't important, but the idea is to prioritize. Third, I ask the agents to reduce their circled values to a top five. Fourth, I ask the agents to put an asterisk by their number one value.

Most of the top-five lists include the values of integrity and/ or honesty. It becomes a leadership credo that influences your agency culture and determines your business reputation. Indeed, character counts—especially when you're dealing with someone's money, risks and hopes. Great leaders have uncompromising values.

Every daily interaction with your team members and customers is a demonstration of your character, which is defined as "moral excellence and firmness." Character enables you and your team to distinguish between right and wrong and then do the right things.

Character is cultivated daily over a lifetime but can be undermined in a single moment by a solitary dishonest action. Hence, you must guard your character with the utmost care—for with it, you're credible, and without it, you're untrustworthy. Once there's an absence of trust, all else is suspect.

It's no coincidence that integrity and honesty are the foundational values of most agencies. If you aren't true to self (integrity), how can you ever be truthful with others (honesty)? If you aren't truthful with others, how can you possibly build a favorable reputation with your team members, customers and community?

Integrity—Being True To Self

We hear so much about integrity that it's often taken for granted—and therein is the danger. Once you and your team assume integrity is a given, breakdowns in character can occur. This is why you should know about the origin of integrity.

General Charles Krulak, a former commandant of the Marine Corps and the leader who instituted values training in boot camp, shared the following story during a standing ovation speech to the Joint Services Conference On Professional Ethics held January 27–28, 2000:

Integrity is a word that comes from the ancient Roman army tradition. During the time of the Twelve Caesars, the Roman army would conduct morning inspections. As the inspecting centurion came in front of each legionnaire, the soldier would strike the armor of his breastplate that covered his heart with his right fist and shout "integritas." That's Latin for material wholeness, completeness and entirety.

The armor over the heart had to be the strongest to protect the soldier from sword thrusts and arrow strikes. The inspecting centurion would listen closely for this affirmation and the ring that well-kept armor would give off.

About this time, the praetorians or imperial bodyguard began to ascend into power and influence. They were drawn from the best "politically correct" soldiers of the legion. They received the finest equipment and armor. They no longer had to shout "integritas" to signify that their armor was sound. Instead, they would shout "Hail Caesar" to signify their heart belonged to the imperial personage. Instead of being true to an institution or code of ideals, their hearts belonged to a single man.

A century passed and the rift between the legionnaires and the imperial guard grew wider. To signify the difference between the two organizations, the legionnaires would no longer shout "integritas" but "integer," which is Latin for undiminished, complete, perfect. It not only indicated that the armor was sound, but also that the soldier was of sound character. His heart was in the right place. He was not associated with the immoral conduct which was rapidly becoming the signature of the praetorian guards.

As a fourth-century Roman general wrote: "When, because of negligence and laziness, parade ground drills were abandoned, the customary armor began to feel heavy since the soldiers rarely, if ever, wore it. Therefore, they first asked the emperor to set aside the breastplates and then the helmets. So our soldiers fought the Goths without any protection for the heart and head, and were often beaten by archers. Although there were many disasters, which led to the loss of great cities, no one tried to restore the armor to the infantry. They took off their armor, and when it came off, so too did their integrity."

General Krulak concluded his speech with these stirring words:

It was only a matter of a few years until the legion rotted within and was unable to hold the frontiers. The barbarians were at the gates. Just as it was true in the days of imperial Rome, you either walk daily in your integrity, or you take off the armor off the "integer" and leave your heart and soul exposed and open to attack.

My challenge to you is simple but often very difficult. Wear your armor of integrity. Take full measure of its weight. Find comfort in its protection. Do not become lax. And always, always remember that no one can take your integrity from you—you, and only you, can give it away!

E. G. Warren, an agent in Gulfport, Mississippi, agrees: "Trust and integrity can never be questioned. It has to be there. I've told my wife many times that she'll never have to worry about my faithfulness. In the same way, I don't want my team members or customers to doubt my integrity and honesty."

Steve Cannon, an agent in Woodstock, Georgia, says: "We don't compromise on our values. To compromise is 'to give up something.' It's impossible to compromise without giving up something. In other words, I must give up something to receive something. In the area of values, compromise is costly. It always corrupts, and then comes the collapse."

Evangelist Billy Graham said it well: "Integrity is the glue that holds our way of life together. When wealth is lost, nothing is lost. When health is lost, something is lost. When character is lost, all is lost."

Former US Senator Alan Simpson advised: "If you have integrity, nothing else matters. If you don't have integrity, nothing else matters."

"Inte**grit**y" includes the word "**grit**," which is defined as "firmness of mind or spirit...unyielding courage." It takes a lot of grit to be true to self. Without integrity, your life is an exercise in deception. Integrity breeds respect, respect leads to influence, and influence produces impact.

Key question: If you were to examine the impact you're having on your team members, customers and community at large, what would it look like?

Honesty—Being Truthful With Others

For the past several years, I've looked forward to receiving a particular monthly issue of a magazine published by a certain insurance company. On the front cover are the names and photos of the company's top ten agents from the previous year. It's an incredible honor since this company is represented by thousands of agents.

In one of these issues, there was a top-ten agent in an area where I was scheduled to speak in about a month. Since I enjoy meeting and talking with top producers, a lunch meeting was arranged. We had an enjoyable conversation, but this agent seemed restless and distracted.

Not long afterward, I learned this agent had been terminated. It seems this top-ten producer had been adding coverage to the policies of existing customers without their permission. What prompted this dishonest behavior? Was it greed? Was it pride? Was it a competitive drive to stay on top?

The good news: This type of moral lapse is the exception, not the rule, at the insurance company this agent once represented. Most agents are the epitome of honesty and integrity. They value their reputation more than anything. They know that doing something unethical or illegal will make them ex-agents. They're unwilling to risk losing their agencies for the sake of more money or greater status.

While honesty is a nonnegotiable character trait in any relationship, it's especially critical in dealing with someone's money, risks and dreams. Nothing will sever a loyal relationship more than a loss of trust. It's trite but true: honesty really is the best policy (pun intended).

Taking it a step further, honesty provides a freedom of mind, body and soul that no dishonest person can ever possess. Honesty means you don't have to remember what you said. Never justify dishonesty by saying, "Everyone else is doing it." Honesty is a long-term investment; the payoff comes in loyal relationships.

Bill Kolb, an agent in Pryor, Oklahoma, states: "Values such as integrity and honesty don't change. It's all about trust. What do you want your customers to say? You're a good salesperson or I trust you. Any organization takes on the values of its leader. This is why you must lead by example. Your bottom line will improve dramatically if your team members and customers know you're a person who can be trusted."

Bill continues: "You can be the greatest salesperson in the world, but if you don't possess certain core values, you won't enjoy long-term success. If you meet the needs of your customers, your needs will be met. If it's all about the money, there will never be enough. Too often everything is driven by the numbers, not needs. I think more agents would be successful if they saw themselves as risk managers, not salespeople."

Chris Dorris, an agent in Hoover, Alabama, says a Top of the Table agent gave him this advice at an MDRT meeting a few years ago: "Stop selling, start listening, tell people the truth, and watch what happens. Your job now becomes your career, and production takes off."

Reputation—Your Character (Or Lack Of It) As Seen By Others

Integrity and honesty determine your reputation. A good reputation is something you can live with; a bad reputation is something you can lose with. A good reputation is like folding a parachute. If the job is done right a thousand times, it's not a story. However, if the job is messed up just once, it's big news.

Likewise, your customers expect you to be trustworthy every time. Should you violate this trust, you'll lose customers, along with any future income and referrals. It reminds me of what Saint Augustine said centuries ago: "When regard for the truth has broken down or even slightly weakened, all things remain doubtful."

One of the things I admire most about Scott Foster is his impeccable reputation. A man of faith, Scott lives out this passage in Proverbs 22:1 (NLT): "Choose a good reputation over great riches, for being held in high esteem is better than having silver or gold." This is why Scott guards his reputation with the utmost care. He knows it determines his credibility or "capacity for belief."

Steve Cannon, an agent in Woodstock, Georgia, says this about reputation protection: "You have three names. The first name is given to you by your parents. The second name is the one that others call you. The third name is the one you make for yourself. Once you lose your name, you won't live long enough to regain it. We live by this credo at our agency: 'Is it right for the customer? Is it right for the company we represent?' If the answer to these two questions is yes, then it's right for us."

It's the reason a reputation is only as good as the values demonstrated daily at your agency. Dan Combs, an agent in Dalton, Georgia, says he and his sixteen team members live by these values:

- We treat everyone with dignity and respect.
- We are dedicated to learning, teaching and ongoing development of each other.
- We have fun while at work.

- We provide a clean, safe environment for our guests and team members.
- We honor individual passions and creativity at work and home.
- We communicate openly, clearly and honesty.
- We honor the relationships that connect our team, our guests and our community.
- We take pride in our commitment to provide remarkable customer service.
- We celebrate and reward accomplishments and "remarkable" players.
- We support balance between home and work.
- We are a profitable and fiscally responsible company.
- We support the physical and emotional well-being of our guests and team members.
- We work as a team through support and cooperation.

In building and protecting your reputation, it's important to understand the difference between image and integrity. Image is what others think you are, and may not be the real you. Integrity is the real you. Many years ago, I learned a powerful lesson about what happens when image and integrity are incongruent.

A company hired me to do a series of seminars for its sales organizations in cities across America. My topic dealt with ethics and professionalism in sales. I was somewhat apprehensive about accepting the opportunity because this industry wasn't a paragon of high moral standards. However, I like a challenge and decided to do my best to make a difference. Fortunately, word spread quickly about the impact this seminar was having on the participants.

One particular day I was in Dallas, Texas, and the room was filled to capacity. A young man said prior to the session: "Mr. Biggs, I flew in from a little town in Arkansas because I've heard good things about your seminar. I just got promoted from salesman to sales manager, and I can't wait to hear what you have to say about ethics and professionalism in sales." My initial image of this young man was that he was serious about learning.

The young sales manager sat on the front row, took copious notes, nodded in agreement and asked thoughtful questions. At the end of the seminar, he shook my hand vigorously and said he planned to share my message with his salespeople. Now, my image of this new sales manager shifted from eager learner to someone who was going to teach what he'd learned to others.

I packed my seminar bag and walked out into the hotel lobby to catch a cab to the airport. The young man from Arkansas spotted me and inquired, "Are you flying out of DFW, Mr. Biggs?" I nodded and he asked, "Well, if you don't have other plans, can we ride together, split the cab fare and talk some more about today's session?" I agreed.

He talked incessantly about the value of ethics and professionalism in sales. He repeated some of the things I'd said. He stressed how valuable the day had been. By the time we arrived at his terminal, my image of this young man had gone from an eager learner willing to share this important message with his salespeople to "Wow, I've really had a big influence on this fellow's life."

The fare was forty dollars. We each paid twenty dollars, but the young man asked the cab driver for a forty-dollar receipt. Pocketing the inflated document, the sales manager winked at me and boasted, "I learned that trick from my general manager." I was speechless, but here's what I was thinking en route to my terminal: (1) What other "tricks" had his general manager taught him?

63

(2) Would he be teaching these "tricks" to his sales force? (3) Had he *heard* anything I'd said that day? Good grief, this was a seminar on ethics and professionalism in sales!

Obviously, my image of this person changed drastically when he failed to be true to himself. He was a man saying one thing and doing another. Regrettably, my message didn't have as much impact on this sales manager as I was led to believe. It also reinforced the fine line between image and integrity.

Audience members often ask these two questions after hearing the cab ride story. First, "Is that really true?" Nah, I just made up a story about integrity. Second, "What's the big deal? He cheated his company out of only twenty dollars." Well, as the late Paul Harvey used to say, you need to hear the "rest of the story" if you think stealing twenty dollars from a company isn't a big deal.

Several years later, and after I had told that story hundreds of times, a woman approached me following a presentation. "Mr. Biggs, I know who that young man is in your cab ride story." She identified the man's name, hometown, industry and employer and told me what had happened to him a few weeks after the seminar.

"That sales manager," she explained, "was bragging to his coworkers about his little trick. It got back to the owner, who fired him on the spot. Can you believe it? That young man lost his job over twenty dollars!"

On the contrary, that Arkansas sales manager lost his job due to a lack of character and failure to understand the difference between image and integrity. Integrity is a unique way of life because it requires being true to self. Never give away your integrity and reputation the way that young man did in Texas years ago.

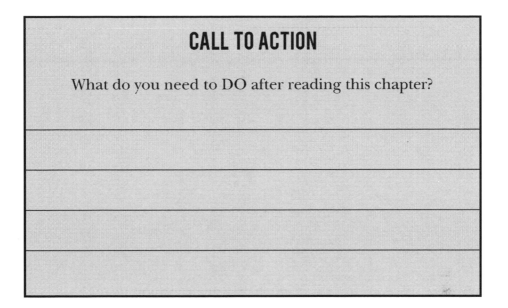

CALL TO ACTION

What do you need to DO after reading this chapter?

TIER 2:
THE TASK-ORIENTED LEADER

It's about the policyholders and sales/service

Succeeding With A System

Going Beyond Goal Setting To Goal Getting

Marketing The Agency

Presenting The Products

Embracing Technology

Chapter 6:
SUCCEEDING WITH A SYSTEM

"Systems are an organized approach to an activity. It's all things
decided in advance and done the same way every time. The
intent is to turn productive activities into routines and habits.
Systems are a means to attack and attain your goals effectively."
–Bill Epperly, *Stoneage Marketing*

Theme:
Are you organized in such a way to achieve optimal results?

Key Points:
- Having a sustainable system
- Favoring sales specialization
- Providing superior service

Jackson Bryan is our thirteen-year-old grandson. He's an eighth-
grader at Palmer Middle School in Kennesaw, Georgia. Palmer has
a program called "Watch Dog," which is for grandfathers who want
to participate with their grandchildren in the school day. I enjoy
attending Jackson's classes, and he likes having me there. Jackson
loves to tell his classmates, "My Papa Dick is a marine!"

As we go from classroom to classroom, I'm impressed with Jackson's high level of organization. His book bag contains two thick
binders full of notes, homework, paper, pencils and other supplies. He has a section for each subject. Everything is filed neatly
and easily accessible. Obviously, Jackson is a lot like his mother,

Tara, a masterful organizer who has a system for everything. I know Jackson and my son-in-law, Bo, appreciate Tara's attention to detail.

Believe it or not, it's a lot easier to be organized than disorganized. Sure, it takes time, self-discipline and hard work to get your agency running smoothly, but it's worth it over the long haul. One of the biggest time wasters is taking too long to get things done because you're ineffective. Looking unorganized, unprepared and unprofessional is no way to operate an agency. Either great leaders are systematic or they hire people who are.

Scott Foster asks, "Every agency has a system, but is it a system for success?" Even a disorganized business is a system, although it's unlikely to produce efficiency and effectiveness. In working with agents since 1990, I've never met a top producer who didn't have an organized and results-oriented system for success. So, are you happy with your current system or does it need an overhaul?

Having A Sustainable System

The Scott Foster Agency revolves around a system of three focus groups: sales, retention and administration. Scott and Mark King, the agency's financial services representative, handle the big life insurance cases and mutual funds within the book of business. Scott's four aspirants— team members who want to become agents—sell outside the agency's book of business.

On the retention side, Scott has four customer service reps who take care of existing customers. Most of these people are long-term employees who are highly skilled in handling service matters and looking for additional sales opportunities. He also has a claims specialist.

Administratively, Scott has two receptionists, two personal assistants and a comptroller. He also has four part-time account contact representatives (ACRs) who do nothing but schedule appointments. Linda, Scott's wife, works part-time handling finances and ordering office supplies. In all, the agency has twenty-one team members.

Scott has an employee manual covering every aspect of agency operations. He says, "It has taken us years to create this manual, and it's constantly evolving." There's a section on agency philosophy, general rules/duties and communication. There's a section on employee benefits, annual reviews and bonuses/contests. There's a section on marketing and goals. There's a section on all product lines. There's a section on claims and emergency instructions.

"Many agents will tell you they're about relationships, not systems," says David Haymon, an agent in Leesville, Louisiana. "They don't have a 'programmer mentality' the way techies do. For instance, I'm good at coming up with ideas, but following up is a weakness. This is why I have one team member who's our 'minister of follow-through.' I don't have to know all the details about our systems, especially when so much is available to us."

E. G. Warren, an agent in Gulfport, Mississippi, concurs: "Our systems run the agency. They should be automatic, but remember: change will occur. It's the only thing that's constant. We're always looking to see if our systems need to be tweaked or completely overhauled. No matter how good our systems are, we must remember that we're in the people business. We need to put a face on doing business with our customers."

P. J. Johnson, an agent in North Charleston, South Carolina, operates her agency with a forty-page employee handbook. It contains her purpose and vision statements, agency policies, commission schedules, tracking procedures and even "how we answer the phone. We're constantly trying to make this handbook better."

Greg Monroe, a field leader in Greenville, North Carolina, recommends a system called the "Power of 240" to his agents. It's based on an average of 20 working days per month. If you multiply 20 by 12 months, that's a total of 240 working days in a year.

Greg explains: "Let's say an agency wants to do 960 auto quotes in a year. This sounds like a really big number. However, if you divide 960 by 240 days, it's a much smaller number—only four auto quotes per day. With this system, an agent can see what happens daily, and a big goal seems more doable. Numbers don't lie."

"Of course," Greg continues, "if you have a bad week or month, it distorts the numbers. Agents must hold the team accountable. There are usually three reasons why an agency isn't hitting its goals: (1) A team member isn't doing his or her daily activities. (2) A team member isn't having the right kinds of conversations with prospects and customers. (3) A team member is making excuses for his or her lack of production—our market is different, our pricing isn't competitive, and so on. If you eliminate the third excuse, the other two usually won't be a problem."

Finally, Greg offers two options to agents who are struggling with meeting their goals. "First, agents need to look at what they're doing wrong and change something. Second, the agency goals may be too ambitious and need to be reduced. I have forty-five-minute conference calls with my agents at the end of each month. Around 90 percent of them participate. We review the daily activities and compare them year-to-date. I also love to tell compelling stories about how agents have made the numbers work."

Ray Cornprobst, a retired field leader in The Villages, Florida, thinks the following systems should in place at every agency:

- **Leadership training**—Do you, the agent, have a plan for growing and getting better?

- **Team development**—Do your team members have a plan for growing and getting better?

- **Visioning**—Does the agency know where it's going in the next five years and beyond?

- **Capacity**—Is your team big enough and competent enough to get the work done?

- **Focus**—Are you and your team concentrating daily on the really important goals?

- **Effective compensation**—Is your pay plan producing the desired results?

- **Follow through for tracking, consistency and accountability**—Are you and your team doing all the little things each day to maximize your opportunities?

- **Communication**—Are you making sure your team is informed about the critical things that will make them successful?

- **Agency growth/production**—Are you monitoring your annual goals against weekly activity?

- **Agency growth/retention**—Are you doing all you can to keep your existing book of business?

- **Customer reviews**—Are you meeting periodically with your customers to go over existing coverage and look for areas of exposure?

- **Referrals**—Are you asking your customers for the names of their family members, friends, neighbors and coworkers who may need your products and services?

Favoring Sales Specialization

If you only have three or four team members, cross-training might be more feasible than specialization. A small team tends to limit the number of products your agency offers. Specialization demands a bigger team because most people can be an expert in only a handful of products.

Many agents say, "I'm already making a great living with a small team. Why should I take on the added headache of a bigger team?" It's because the more products you have in a household, the more likely you'll be viewed as an insurance and financial services resource, making it less attractive for your customers to go elsewhere. When you're perceived as a commodity, particularly in property and casualty, you run a greater risk of losing your customers to aggressive competition.

Renewal income is a wonderful thing, but it can fuel complacency by luring you into in a comfort zone. It's often a subtle process. You become content with a certain income and miss out on the joy of cultivating a dream team capable of taking care of your customers in all areas of insurance and financial services. This transcends making more money to making a meaningful, memorable difference in the lives of your team members and customers.

"One of the best things about specialization," says Denis Husers, a retired field leader in Lake Charles, Louisiana, "is that it enables the team to do a better job of multi-lining. The more products you have in a household, the better your customer loyalty. When you have at least three or four products in a household, there's a very slim chance of losing this customer unless you run into an underwriting problem or some other special situation."

Sully Blair, an agent in Bennettsville, South Carolina, is a big proponent of specialization. "I worked for an agent and did everything. I thought it was the best way at the time. We only saw our agent one day in the seven and a half years I was a team member. It has been a tough transition to specialization, but it's the better way. I identify the strengths of each team member and put people where they'll excel. I don't want any team member doing more than two or three things well."

David Wilcox, an agent in Gonzales, Louisiana, sees specialization differently. "Every team member can sell anything, but we have a team captain who is the 'go-to' person for each product line. Our service team members can also sell. My three aspirants specialize in auto, home and life but have no service responsibilities."

Terri Brock, an agent in Columbia, South Carolina, admits: "I fought specialization for a while but now believe that it's the best system. No one can be an expert on everything, so it just makes more sense to specialize. Perhaps the only drawback is if a particular specialist departs, it creates a temporary strain on the rest of the team until we can find a replacement. I once had a life and health specialist leave, which meant we had to scramble to get up-to-date on these two products."

Fact: Experts don't have to know everything about a particular product; they just have to know more than the people they're talking to. To be an authentic expert in a particular product, you must truly believe in it. The best way to believe in a product is to own it.

David Vanderzee, a member of MDRT's Top of the Table, wrote in *Advisor Today*, "I've found that agents have a hard time selling with conviction something they haven't bought themselves and made a long-term commitment to."

Providing Superior Service

A great agency is more concerned with keeping promises than making promises. After all, a policy is simply a promissory piece of paper for a potential claim. Obviously, an insurance company is bound by law to make good on the policy's stipulated promises, but isn't it how these promises are kept that make or break your agency's reputation? This is why superior service can't be just a slogan; it has to be a credible, habitual way of doing business.

Dan Combs, an agent in Dalton, Georgia, takes this approach: "Superior service is all about urgency and execution. We treat customer care like something that's on fire. I have a special file marked 'second requests' and it's empty. This means action is being taken the minute it hits someone's desk—and that's the way we like it."

One of the best ways to provide superior service is to do periodic customer reviews. According to Ray Cornprobst, a retired field leader in The Villages, Florida, "the money isn't in reviewing the existing policies of your customers. It's about retention. The sale is keeping a customer for another year. Sure, these reviews will produce sales, but the real benefit is staying in touch with your customers so they perceive your agency as a valuable resource."

Unfortunately, many agents get complacent about doing these periodic reviews, which can lead to perilous consequences. For example, a friend of mine maintained his auto and home insurance with one agent for twenty years. When I asked why he left, my friend said, "No one ever called me in twenty years. I felt like my agent didn't care or appreciate my business."

He continued: "A new guy happened to join our golf group and he was always asking questions about my family and business. I knew there were other insurance products my family and growing business probably needed, but my longtime agent never discussed these matters with me. Turns out my new golfing buddy was an insurance agent. Eventually, he met with us to review our entire range of risks. Besides taking over our auto and home policies, this agent also helped us with our life insurance, our business insurance and some investments."

Thinking about this scenario prompted these questions: Did the former agent assume my friend would never leave him? (Probably.) Was the former agent simply content living off his renewals from my friend? (Likely.) Did the former agent miss out on additional ways to help my friend? (Definitely.)

When I asked my friend about his dissatisfaction with his previous agent, he replied: "I would have loved it if my longtime agent had done these periodic reviews. In fact, it's the primary reason I went elsewhere. My new agent now makes me feel the way I wanted to feel all those years I was with the other agent."

If you're really sincere about providing superior service, don't you owe it to every policyholder to offer a periodic review? It's an opportunity to tell policyholders how much you value their business and loyalty. It's a chance to look for areas of exposure. It's an occasion to create multiple sales in a household, making it less attractive for a policyholder to leave while maximizing your renewals.

Of course, this free service is time-consuming, requires ongoing learning and might create a need for a team of specialists. What's the alternative? You could lose loyal policyholders and a lot of future income by *assuming* they'll never leave your agency.

Scott Foster is a big believer in these periodic reviews. These meetings are arranged mostly by his account contact representatives (ACRs). "Most customers won't give us an hour for this review, but we've found they're more likely to meet with us if we suggest a forty-five-minute appointment. The last thing we want to do is waste the valuable time of our customers."

Typically, Scott spends about fifteen minutes going over existing policies and the rest of the time talking about any uncovered risks. Depending upon what needs are discovered and the interest level of the customer, Scott might call in one of his product specialists to join the conversation. To help Scott identify any particular needs, his receptionist has already asked the customer to complete a one-page "client profile" before the meeting:

HELP US HELP YOU! by completing the following:

**Indicate the level of importance to
you at this time in your life:**   **High**   **Medium** **Low**

Knowing you won't outlive your
retirement savings   ____   ____   ____

Having enough money to retire comfortably ____   ____   ____

Rolling an old 401(k)/retirement plan
into a current plan   ____   ____   ____

Having enough money to pay for your
children's education   ____   ____   ____

Having enough money to pay off the
mortgage and debts and provide income
to your family in case of death   ____   ____   ____

Having money to pay bills if you
cannot work due to an illness/injury   ____   ____   ____

Being able to pay for the cost
of long-term care   ____   ____   ____

Reducing the cost of health insurance
for your family   ____   ____   ____

Having comprehensive coverage for jewelry
and other items that have limited
coverage under a homeowner's policy   ____   ____   ____

Lowering your monthly car payment   ____   ____   ____

Finding a better interest rate for
your savings/CDs   ____   ____   ____

Having financial protection from lawsuits ____   ____   ____

Protecting your business
(property and liability)   ____   ____   ____

This form also has space for the client's name, spouse's name, dependents, telephone numbers, email addresses, emergency contact information and the date of the review.

Kirk Baker, an agent in Valencia, California, is also an advocate of the customer review, but he takes a different approach. "I use a 50-inch television monitor and an Excel spreadsheet to do what I call an asset review. The focus is on liability exposure, particularly in big cases. Since I've already seen their assets and income, it's a soft transition into financial services. It changes the entire dynamic of the relationship because it might take two or three more appointments to come up with the right solutions. We're no longer viewed as a commodity."

To provide superior service, you and your team must be the best professionals possible. Get excited about all the opportunities you have to help your customers. Take the time to stay in touch with the people that make your agency possible. Let them know about all the ways you can be of service. Be perceived as a valuable resource that cares about the needs of your customers. Above all, beware the perils of complacency.

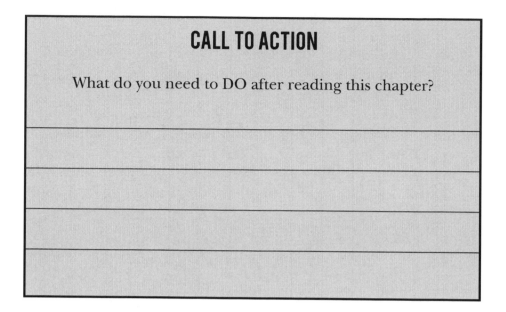

CALL TO ACTION

What do you need to DO after reading this chapter?

Chapter 7:

GOING BEYOND GOAL SETTING TO GOAL GETTING

"The most successful businesses are those that have some type of written plan (read: goals). There is power in a well-written plan."
–Mark LeBlanc, *Growing Your Business*

Theme:
Are you turning the annual business plan into a living, breathing document every day?

Key Points:
- *Why* do your plan?
- *What* goes into your plan?
- *How* does your plan become a reality?

I co-founded the Chattahoochee Road Runners with Ron Creasy and Ron Varner in 1981. I'd already run two marathons but wanted to improve my time with the help of some training partners. Our club grew rapidly, and I got to know a lot of our members. I surveyed the ones with marathon times faster than mine. After digesting their suggestions, I developed an annual training regimen and followed it relentlessly for five years.

During this period, my time in this 26.2-mile race improved from four hours, forty-three minutes and forty-six seconds to a personal record of three hours, nineteen minutes and forty-seven seconds at the Rocket City Marathon in Huntsville, Alabama. **Lesson learned:** While goal setting is a powerful self-motivator, goal getting requires a systematic game plan that must be implemented consistently if success is to be achieved.

Regardless of your agency production level, how much better could it be with a well-conceived annual business plan? Just as I consulted with marathon runners who were better than me, why wouldn't you do the same with agents who are more successful than you? Once you've garnered their pearls of wisdom, develop a dynamic business plan and implement it daily, weekly and monthly in the pursuit of your annual goals. Repeat this process year after year and you have a recipe for prolonged success.

Fact: Great leaders are purposeful planners. To help you with this process, here's my 7Rs system to go beyond goal setting to goal getting:

Respectable—If your goals aren't aligned with the high standards of the agency purpose statement, why pursue them?

Realistic—Set everyone up to succeed by pursuing fewer, realistic goals. As confidence is gained and momentum is created, go after loftier ambitions.

Record—Written goals provide better accountability. Many studies prove why success increases when goals are put on paper.

Reduce to the specific—Don't say, "I want to sell more this year." Be specific: "I want to write fifty life insurance policies on or before December 31."

Reflect upon often—Visualize the attainment of your goals. This provides constant *mental* reinforcement so you can maintain the intensity of your focus.

Relentlessly pursue—Nothing happens without *physical* effort, so go for your goals with gusto.

Responsibility—No matter how goal driven you are, life is unpredictable. There will be times when you'll have to postpone some or all your goals due to the illness of a loved one, health problems and so on. When the time is right, resume the quest for your goals or reassess what you want to accomplish.

Why Do Your Plan?

Can your agency do well without having a business plan each year? Sure, but a written plan increases your chances for success by:

- providing measurable short-term progression toward the agency's long-term vision
- creating greater clarity because everyone knows what the agency goals are
- offering constant reinforcement when the agency goals are posted in prominent places
- stimulating a healthy state of urgency and competition among the team
- increasing accountability because there's a written record of the stated intentions.

I once heard someone say how he and his wife spent a great deal of time creating a lengthy list of their long-term goals. This list ended up in the glove box of their car and wasn't retrieved until years later when they traded for a new model. Even though they hadn't looked at this list for a few years, these goals were etched clearly in their minds because they'd put them in writing. Turns out they'd achieved about half of the goals on their list. Can you imagine what would have happened if these goals had remained in sight?

Indeed, the habit of writing down your goals is a powerful exercise. It's a big part of making time to think about your agency and where you're headed. At my age, if I don't write things down, good ideas tend to vanish more quickly than a slow wildebeest being stalked by a fleet lion on an African plain. Even if you have an excellent memory, it's unlikely that you'll remember every agency goal when there are so many other things you have to deal with daily. In short, a written plan is more reliable.

Stan Simmons, an agent in Lawrenceburg, Kentucky, prefers an annual theme for his business plan. One year it was "Keeping The Right Focus," a gentle reminder for the team to keep an eye on the agency goals. Another year it was "Flood Warning," a way to prompt the team to help as many clients as possible with their needs: The flood gates are open. The sky's the limit!

Scott Foster is so focused on goals that he has a dedicated section on this topic in his employee manual. He says, "Our success is a direct result of the goals we set and the plans we have for reaching them. Each team member will have specific goals. Each team member will document progress toward achieving his or her individual goals. Your progress will be an important part of your performance review."

Phil Nichols, an agent in Knoxville, Tennessee, states: "Some things haven't changed. You have to have goals, a track to run on. More importantly, you need the passion to achieve your goals. We're all about goal implementing. We're especially big on making MDRT and being consistent in our production. I'm blessed to have fourteen loyal team members who are dedicated to helping us reach our goals and grow the agency."

Dave Wilcox, an agent in Gonzales, Louisiana, suggests a "planning conference toward the end of the year to map your direction for the following year. I'm an old high school football coach and it's all about preparation. You can't just set goals; you need strategies for reaching them. And you have to execute. It takes practice, practice, practice."

P. J. Johnson, an agent in North Charleston, South Carolina, states: "That which gets monitored gets done. This is a business, so you need a plan. A good plan also needs good metrics. I've had a P&L since day one. You have to know where your money is going. I can tell you line by line how much I'm spending—and on what. I know our percentage of growth by product line year by year."

What Goes Into Your Plan?

There are a lot of ways to do an annual business plan. If your method is working, keep it up. If you're looking for some ways to make your plan more exciting, here are some tips:

- Is your vision statement included in the plan? If you want the agency to be at a certain level in the next five years and beyond, you need to be reminded of the big picture every year.
- What are the overall business strategies for growing the agency?
- What are the specific goals for the agent and each team member? How do these goals fit into the overall agency projections?
- What are the action plans for achieving these goals? What role will each team member play in attaining these goals?

- What are the financial projections in terms of income, expenses and profit? What about capital expenditures on your facility? What about hiring new team members?
- What are the personal goals of the agent?
- What are the personal goals of each team member?

These are the basic elements of a sound annual business plan. How long should it be? Long enough to get the job done. I've seen annual business plans ranging from one page to more than two hundred pages. **My advice:** Less is often more. Somewhere between fifteen and thirty pages should be a sufficient length for most agencies.

Consider having an annual agency planning retreat in late November or early December. Celebrate the successes of the current year and forecast your plans for the following year. All team members should work on their goals prior to the meeting. Use the retreat to coordinate everything into a synchronized plan to create excitement for the plan's execution.

How Does Your Plan Become A Reality?

Johanna Kelly, a field leader in Binghamton, New York, offers this advice: "Agents need to take some private time to focus on their business plans. They should define their goals against reality. They should develop an achievable plan they're committed to. They should be able to adjust as needed throughout the year."

Unfortunately, a lot of agents dread doing the annual business plan. Some simply change the date on the plan each year. Some do a half-hearted plan, which is soon filed and forgotten. Some rationalize why a plan is even needed and do nothing.

Sam Eubank, a field leader in Newburgh, New York, says: "If you ask team members if the agency had a good or bad month, a lot of them don't know. They're lost in the process. This often leads to frustration and higher turnover. That's why it's crucial to review the annual goals against weekly production. If there are gaps between these two areas, you adapt, provide needed training and remind the team of their roles in accomplishing the agency goals and staying aligned with the agency vision."

I'm reminded of an Ohio field leader who hired me to speak to her agents several years ago. She asked, "Is there a way for my agents to turn the annual business plan into a living, breathing document?" I called this leader a couple weeks later and shared a four-part plan on how to "turn the annual business plan into a living, breathing document." I've been sharing the following strategy with agents ever since:

Mastermind the plan annually. Take a creative look at the agency goals every year and make sure each team member is committed to his or her achievement. Finalize the business plan at your annual agency planning retreat.

Maximize the plan daily. This means chipping away habitually at the annual goals. It requires an intentional effort to make the calls, set the appointments, complete the applications and follow up as needed. Daily prioritization turns into weekly production, consistent weekly production enables your agency to reach its annual goals, and consistent annual production allows the agency to realize its vision.

Monitor the plan weekly. This should be a two-way forum of exchange at your agency meetings: (1) Team members give progress reports. (2) You provide inspiration, positive feedback and accountability.

Measure the plan quarterly. This is a time for recognition and reward. Make it a fun celebration—music, balloons, food, guest speaker or whatever it takes to create a festive occasion. It's also a good time to review the agency purpose, vision and annual goals.

Todd Jackson, an agent in Anchorage, Alaska, takes an innovative approach to masterminding the plan annually and maximizing the plan daily. "First, I sit with each team member and have a conversation about his or her annual goals. Instead of a wish list, I want it to be a realistic projection of the numbers each member intends to hit. Also, team members must understand the consequences for not meeting their objectives, most notably a loss in compensation. In other words, I want to know if they're truly committed to achieving their goals."

"Second," Todd says, "we all have a daily business plan on our desks. It's focused on leading indicators (activity) versus lagging indicators (actual production). It's a one-page document focused on calls, quotes and so on. We find that if this activity is done consistently every day, production follows. This simple system has made all the difference in our office." **Note:** Todd has been a top-ten agent three times at the company he represents.

Denis Husers, a retired field leader in Lake Charles, Louisiana, believes in monitoring the plan weekly. "I've always subscribed to the 'it's a cinch by the inch' philosophy. Set weekly goals, have weekly payoffs and celebrate your success. Most teams thrive on this approach because the goals are more manageable by the week. It's not just about the monetary rewards; recognition and appreciation go a long way in keeping the team focused on its goals."

Greg Monroe, a field leader in Greenville, North Carolina, says this about measuring the plan: "Team members are the most powerful group in our profession. These people do the daily activities necessary to take the business plan from inception to implementation. You want to do everything possible to celebrate with the people who help you reach your agency goals."

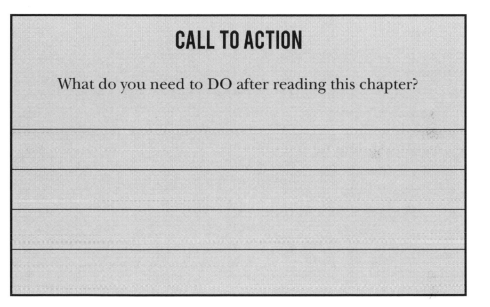

CALL TO ACTION

What do you need to DO after reading this chapter?

Chapter 8:

MARKETING THE AGENCY

"Marketing is not a department. It's your business. Every act is a marketing act. Make every employee a marketing person."
–Harry Beckwith, *Selling The Invisible*

Theme:
Are you positioning the agency to take full advantage of all available opportunities?

Key Points:
- Marketing-selling marriage
- Managing the marketing mix
- Making the monetary commitment

So often in my career, aspiring speakers have offered to "pick my brain" over a meal. They rave about their superb communication skills. They boast about being an expert in a particular field. To this, I always ask: "But can you market your business? Because if you can't, the main thing you'll be doing is practicing your program in front of the bedroom mirror and wondering why you don't have any engagements. The most dynamic presentation in the world is worthless if no one knows about it."

Of course, no amount of marketing will offset poor performance. The story is told of an aspiring speaker who created an expensive marketing brochure, including a long list of reasons for hiring him. Within the year, this speaker was broke and out of business.

When someone asked a meeting planner why the slick brochure speaker didn't make it, she replied, "Oh, it was his dreadful word-of-mouth that killed him!"

Obviously, it takes more than a clever marketing program to succeed in business. At your agency, you need a competent, action-oriented team of sales, service and administrative specialists who understand that marketing is a part of every job description. You're being judged daily on how marketing promises are kept. Regardless of your agency title, every interaction with a prospect or customer is an opportunity to gain a new account, retain an old one or secure referrals. In short, favorable agency word-of-mouth is the best marketing you can possibly have.

Marketing-Selling Marriage

Marketing and selling are like a good marriage. While there are differences between a husband and wife, they form a formidable team when they work together. Likewise, for an agency to succeed, marketing and selling should be compatible, even though there are major differences between the two concepts:

- Marketing is about the message. Selling is about the messengers who represent the products and services proclaimed by the message.
- Marketing is what you do to keep your products and services in front of prospects and clients so they think of you when they're ready to buy. Selling is the exchange of money for a product or service.
- Marketing isn't about whom you know; it's about who knows you! Selling isn't about high-pressure tactics; it's about hassle-free problem solving.

- Marketing requires a capital outlay and usually takes a lot of time. Selling should make you money and often occurs in a brief time span, like the stroke of a pen or nod of the head.
- Marketing establishes your brand, or who you are in the marketplace. Selling extols the benefits of how your products will fulfill needs.

Tom Wright, an agent in Porterville, California, and author of *Stop Selling & Start Marketing,* says: "Marketing is a way to reach out to customers who want to be reached. Marketing is a planned approach whereby you locate people who have a propensity to need your product or service and help them fill their needs. A planned, repeatable marketing program allows your organization to market on a perpetual basis. Marketing is an organized program, not a project you do once a month until you meet a quota."

"The challenge," Tom maintains, "is not selling something to someone. It's about developing a way to have clients want to come to us to fulfill or satisfy their needs. Over the years, I've found there are two types of sales that are made. One is through persuasion, in which the salesperson convinces the prospect that he or she needs a product or service. The other is not really a sale at all but rather a fulfillment of the prospect's needs."

Tom likes to find a group of prospects who have a particular need. He sends out preapproach letters. A team member follows up with a phone call: "Tom would like to meet with you concerning your life insurance needs. He's available next Tuesday or Thursday. Which of these dates is more convenient?"

"The key," says Tom "is to reference me in the letter so that the team members don't lose confidence due to rejection. Once the appointment is made, 90 percent of the work is done. It's simply a matter of being prepared for the appointment."

Tom has his team prepare a file with various proposals to meet a prospect's needs. He reaches for this file as he ushers the prospect into his office and says with a laugh, "'What brings you in today?' It's all about the customer, and having fun in the process. Instead of pushing a product, I prefer a counseling mode. I want to build a relationship. I want to be perceived as a resource who adds value. It's a subtle but highly professional, effective approach."

Great agency leaders understand the importance of superb marketing and selling. The two concepts are a skillful blend of prospect identification and needs clarification for the mutual benefit of the customer and agency. While there's no substitute for sales skills, it all begins with masterful marketing so prospects think of your agency when they're ready to do business.

Managing The Marketing Mix

Nido Qubein, president of High Point University in High Point, North Carolina, said at a National Speakers Association many years ago, "The magic of marketing is in the mix." If I've learned anything about marketing as a business owner since 1982, it's this: There are many ways to reach prospects. The key is to track what works and keep using it for a sustained period of time.

Jim Cornwell, an agent in Tampa, Florida, agrees: "I've always taken a mixed approach to marketing. The key is to be consistent—a minimum of two years. There's no one thing that works. Rather, it's a combination of things. We use direct mail. We have our name on bus shelters. We partner with schools and our banner is displayed at the front entrance. We have our name on grocery bags, which has been a big hit. We have a marketing budget each year. We track results. If something is getting stale, we're not afraid to make changes."

Sully Blair, an agent in Bennettsville, South Carolina, says: "I'm on six billboards in our town of ten thousand people, so I guess you could say I'm a local celebrity. My face is seen at all six major arteries in Bennettsville. We're also real big on asking for referrals after every sale. We pass out these little cards that say, 'The best thing you can do for me is a referral.'"

Perhaps Sully's best marketing strategy is an arrangement he has with some local restaurants. He gives his customers something resembling a business card. In reality, it's a free lunch card expressing Sully's appreciation for doing business with his agency. He gets billed monthly by the restaurant owners. "The tab usually runs around $1,000–$1,500 per month, but it's worth every penny. Incidentally, we have all the personal and business insurance of these restaurant owners."

Another strategy used by Sully is handwritten notes. "I do them every Monday morning to customers who are about to get renewal notices. I thank them for their business and include a couple of free lunch tickets. Even if a rate increase is coming, we don't lose many customers because they know we value their business."

"You can't catch a fish if you don't wet the hook," proclaims P. J. Johnson, an agent in North Charleston, South Carolina. "My photo is on the billboard at the airport gateway. We have our message on newspaper sticky notes. We do banner ads on the Weather Bug and ESPN. We're active on Facebook. I troll life events such as anniversaries, birthdays and so on. I ping my congratulations and ask them to call me. It works."

Dan Combs, an agent in Dalton, Georgia, believes "marketing is what makes production possible. We have a huge market presence in our city and Whitfield County, an area of 110,000 people. We love sponsorships of all kinds. We're on billboards. We're on talk shows with our local cable station. We even participated in a national ad for the company I represent."

"We're big on Internet leads," says Perry Olson, an agent with locations in Las Vegas and Henderson, Nevada. "A lot of agents think this produces a lot of junk business, but we write six to seven hundred apps a month. We use the following six-step process with our quotes:

- Call the prospect and give them the price quote up front.
- Text the prospect. A special template outlines the coverage and price breakdown.
- Email the prospect with the price in the subject line.
- Mail the prospect using a special red envelope.
- Setup a strategic marketing plan (SMP) that automatically contacts the prospect.
- Call two days later. This is done by another person dedicated to follow-up calls."

Making The Monetary Commitment

Scott Foster's agency is a relentless marketer. Everything is done tastefully but persistently. As multiline customers, Judy and I receive old-fashioned snail mail letters, email newsletters, cards for special occasions, telephone calls on our birthdays, calendars in December and more. It's hard to forget someone who is so consistent.

Scott knows he has to spend money to make money. For example, longtime customers are given a tote bag full of goodies—a small whiteboard to affix to their refrigerator, an ice cream scoop, a chip clip, an umbrella, a coffee mug, a road atlas, sticky notes, a pedometer and more. Naturally, Scott's name and contact information are embossed on each item.

Al Clark, a perennial number one agent in Arlington, Texas, says in *Al Clark's Multi-Million Dollar Formula 4 Success*: "I decided it would be more profitable to grow the business through marketing. I call it making the business work when you aren't physically working. The four most important marketing secrets are: (1) Think of your marketing plan as an investment. (2) Be committed to your plan. (3) Be consistent with your plan. (4) Have a systematic process for your plan."

Sam Eubank, a field leader in Newburgh, New York, says: "It's typical for an agent to spend at least $3,000–$4,000 per month on marketing. Early on, most of the money should be allocated to lead generation, not branding. Once renewal income starts coming in, an agent can devote more money to branding, like being on a menu at the local diner and so on. Most of all, an agent must understand where the money is going and be able to track the results."

P. J. Johnson, an agent in North Charleston, South Carolina, has a monthly marketing budget of $6,000. "It's about top-of-mind presence in the marketplace. You have to invest on the front end to get a back-end return. We're on billboards. We have a kiosk in the local mall and do live quoting."

P. J. adds: "We're on scorecards at three golf courses. Who plays golf? Rich people! So we market financial services to these people. We do some direct mail. We buy Internet leads. We sponsor Little League teams, but only if they invite us to the first meeting of the parents. We want them to know the person who's on that T-shirt."

Stan Simmons, an agent in Lawrenceburg, Kentucky, says: "Making a monetary commitment in marketing is the foundation of any agency success. We hired a marketing representative to make sure we get the full penetration of sales in Anderson County. We set aside 12 percent as a marketing budget, not including the compensation for our marketing rep."

Matt Schomburg, an agent in Katy, Texas, states: "Many agents see marketing as a cost or expense, but it's really a long-term commitment for growing your agency. I started a company car program in 2004. If a team member has been with me for three years, he or she gets a car. I have ten cars in my fleet and nine of them have those ridiculous vehicle wraps. My young team members drive these cars all over town—ball games, schools, restaurants and churches—so it's a rolling billboard of advertisement for us.

"It's an expensive program, but every car is paid for. I haven't lost a team member I wanted to keep since launching the car program. I pay for everything except gas. I even have a remote team member in Kerrville, which is four hours away. I've had agents call to ask why one of my cars is in Kerrville. I'm licensed in Texas, so it's opened up another market for us.

"Most of all, vehicle-wrap marketing gives us tremendous presence in our community. I was in my workout clothes one day while buying something. The salesman rang up the order and asked for my frequent shopper card. I didn't have it with me, so the salesman said he'd look it up under my name. When I told him, the salesman exclaimed, '*THE* Matt Schomburg? I can't wait to tell everyone I met you!'"

Matt believes another way to have market visibility is to give back to your community. "I became a board member at our local YMCA five years ago. I chaired our fund-raising campaign for two years before being asked to serve as board chairman. I've met a lot of tremendous people. All this exposure caused our local newspaper to call concerning our relocation to a 12,000-square-foot strip mall, where I have six tenants."

Finally, to understand the importance of marketing, here's what Richard Weylman, a professional speaker and marketing guru based in Punta Gorda, Florida, says in *Opening Closed Doors*: "People don't fail because they can't sell or have nothing to sell; they fail because they didn't have access to enough buyers."

CALL TO ACTION

What do you need to DO after reading this chapter?

Chapter 9

PRESENTING THE PRODUCTS

"Know your business well enough so you're right at home no
matter what the prospect brings up."
–Ben Feldman, *The Feldman Method*

Theme:

Are you having the hard conversations with your customers to
minimize their exposure to major risks?

Key Points:

- Having enough appointments
- Educating enough people
- Submitting enough applications

David Haymon is an agent in Leesburg, Louisiana. Prior to agency,
David was a field leader in Columbia, Missouri. During his time in
"The Show Me State," David's mother suffered a serious injury in
a car accident. Fortunately, David's father, Gene, an agent who's
since retired, had the right health coverage on his wife. The high
cost of treatment and recovery were covered. It prompted David
to write an article entitled "Why Are You Here?" and send it to his
agents:

*Why are you here? You may not ponder this question very much, but I
encourage you to do so in thinking about how you'll operate in the coming
year. Never before has this question hit home with such impact as after the
recent accident and injuries sustained by my mother. Hopefully, it will be a*

once-in-a-lifetime occurrence for us. Unfortunately, these once-in-a-lifetime things happen every day to the people we insure.

My family has been blessed in many ways concerning this accident. First, we could have lost three family members. Second, my mother's injuries could have been much worse. Third, my family hasn't had to worry about where the money is coming from to pay for the surgery, ambulance rides, hospital bills, inpatient rehabilitation bills and the upcoming home health care/ outpatient rehabilitation. Unless you've had a similar experience, you can't fathom how much this means to a family to not have to worry about these expenses.

So I ask: If my family were insured with you, would we have had the conversations necessary to ensure the same coverage was in force? Would you be able to tell me how these discussions and recommendations were going to provide the needed care? Or would you be making excuses for why these conversations hadn't occurred? Would you be explaining why there's no coverage for these unexpected expenses? These are serious questions with serious repercussions.

It's not really about production levels, although this is the best gauge we have for it. It IS about having meaningful conversations with EVERY policyholder. It IS about taking an initial objection and addressing it. It IS about having a potentially uncomfortable conversation now to ensure that you don't have to have one after an accident.

If you need a reason why hospital income, disability, long-term care, life and liability conversations HAVE to take place, contact me and I'll give you a whopper of a tale that's 100 percent true. If you aren't interested in this conversation, then I return to my original question: Why are you here?

E. G. Warren, an agent in Gulfport, Mississippi, agrees with this approach. "Stories really resonate with our customers. For instance, we have eight hundred life insurance policies in force, so we've paid a lot of death claims, including at least one every month last year. Customers can identify with stories that happened in their neighborhood. It makes what we do very real."

Having Enough Appointments

Scott Foster calls it the "law of big numbers." You can't educate enough people and submit enough applications if you don't have enough appointments. The key to securing enough appointments is making enough contacts. The way Scott does this at his agency is by having four part-time account contact representatives (ACRs) on his agency team. Many of them are high school or college students who are eager to earn an income.

Scott's ACRs work twelve to fifteen hours each week arranging face-to-face appointments. Because this work can be grueling, Scott prefers part-time ACRs to maximize productivity and minimize burnout. He pays his ACRs $8 per hour, plus $5 for each appointment that shows up, and another $5 if a sale is made. Do the math. His ACRs can earn up to $18 per hour if they're really good.

Mark King, Scott's longtime financial services representative, shared this observation: "If I had to name just one common denominator of mature, successful agencies, it would be appointment activity. You have to work your book of business. You have to be proactive in looking for new sales opportunities and increasing retention. For us, nothing works better than having periodic reviews with our customers."

"I take an old-school approach with our customers," says Dave Munson, an agent in Ellicott City, Maryland. "We help them understand why it's important to have a personal relationship with their agency team. We believe in customer service, including periodic customer reviews. We tell customers why it's important to protect the most important thing they have—their lives. About 30 percent of our households have life insurance. We've delivered a lot of death claims in my nineteen-year career and no one ever complains about getting that check."

Dave makes a good point. The only people who say they're "insurance poor" are the ones who've never received a claim check. So the next time you get the "insurance poor" objection while trying to set an appointment, gently remind your prospects that what you do is life changing. People have car accidents every day. People lose their homes in fires and storms every day. People get hurt on the job every day. People retire every day. People go into nursing homes every day. And yes, people die every day.

Denis Husers, a retired field leader in Lake Charles, Louisiana, says: "You don't have to be a great salesperson to be successful in the insurance and financial services profession; you just need to have enough appointments. If you do that, the sales will take care of themselves because 90 percent of the people you talk to need something you're offering. They can't buy if you don't tell them. You never want customers saying they'd have bought a product if they'd just known about it."

Educating Enough People

A California field leader has this sales philosophy: "Products don't sell; benefits do. Agencies should have a benefit statement for each product. The key to success is having a team that knows these benefits and uses them. They should also state what coverage is available for each of these products. When you get resistance, tell stories about customers who didn't have certain coverage and the impact it had on their financial situation. Or tell stories about customers who had certain coverage and the difference it made in their lives."

Bill Kolb, an agent in Pryor, Oklahoma, believes salesmanship is vastly overrated. "Customers are too smart for all of these canned responses to objections. It's all about building trust with the customer. Are you selling or telling? You tend to sell when you're not confident in your products. When you know you have competitive products, just tell your customers what you have to offer based on their needs."

Bill goes on: "Once you discover the needs of your customers, advise what products will solve their problems. Customers need advice, not salesmanship. When I go to my CPA, attorney or dentist, they don't try to sell me on what needs to be done. They tell me. They advise me. When you do this, you'll be satisfied with every transaction regardless of the outcome."

Scott Foster thinks there's no better way to believe in a product than to own it personally. Scott made MDRT his first year in the business by selling 122 life policies. At that time, Scott owned $100,000 of whole life insurance—a decent amount in the early 1970s. At a breakfast meeting during his first MDRT convention in San Francisco, California, Scott had the good fortune to sit across the table from Ben Feldman, a legendary life insurance agent in the twentieth century.

After some small talk, Ben asked Scott how much life insurance he owned. Scott proudly told Mr. Feldman he had $100,000 of whole life insurance. Ben looked directly at Scott and asked, "If you died tomorrow, would you want your wife to live on $100,000 for the rest of her life?" Scott went home and purchased a sizeable amount of additional permanent life insurance. It's no coincidence that Scott's consistently high life production over many years is tied directly to his belief in the product.

Stan Simmons, an agent in Lawrenceburg, Kentucky, has a "Service Plus One" approach: "After taking care of customers' needs, we ask them about ONE other product they don't have with us. We don't ask them about EVERY product because we have so many in our toolbox. In this way, we let our customers know we care and can help them in many ways. It works."

Bill Thorp, an agent in Grants Pass, Oregon, states: "It's all about educating customers concerning their needs. Present products that make sense and offer them three choices. If you see them nodding their heads in agreement, it will be hard for them to nod no when it's time to make a decision. All you've got is trust and faith with your customers, which comes more through educating than selling."

Tom Davis, an agent in Oxford, Mississippi, believes "it's all about a conversation. I take a very laid-back approach to educating people. I ask a lot of questions. I make recommendations based on someone's needs. I like to keep it simple. If you do enough educating, the apps and sales will follow."

Submitting Enough Applications

Art Brucks, an agent in Burleson, Texas, compares playing softball to meeting with customers and obtaining their business. In an article entitled "Square Up, Look Mean, Swing Hard," Art says he pounded this approach into his daughter Rebecca's head when she was a softball player.

"Square up means getting your feet, body and bat in the correct position…your back straight, rear end out and hands up. Look mean is about getting rid of any distractions and focusing intently on the pitcher and the ball as it's delivered. Swing hard is being confident and giving it your best shot with every at-bat."

Art then asks: "Couldn't we use this same approach in sales situations? Square up means creating the right environment for success. Be prepared with your proposals. Be knowledgeable about your products. Have your paperwork organized. Look mean is about getting your game face on and giving the best professional advice possible. Swing hard relates to identifying needs and asking for the order. Either customers buy what you're telling them, or you buy the reasons why they won't give you a check. You won't make every sell, but you'll certainly improve your batting average by following this routine."

Gary Welch, an agent in Peoria, Illinois, has a relaxed approach to production. "I like to have three face-to-face appointments with customers each day. My goal is to inform, educate and offer solutions. I review existing policies and make certain recommendations. I don't want a customer to ever say I didn't provide the information necessary to make important decisions. Otherwise, I'm vulnerable, particularly in an area like life insurance."

Gary continues: "As I do these reviews with customers, I'm looking at my notes from the last meeting. If I notice we talked about certain gaps in their coverage, it gives me an opportunity to ask why they haven't acted and answer any questions they may have. At the end of the day, my focus isn't on an app count, but rather on what kind of job I did in educating my customers. That's how I define productivity."

105

"Tracking apps, sales and premium are lagging indicators," asserts Ray Cornprobst, a retired field leader in The Villages, Florida. "I'm a proponent of tracking leading indicators such as appointments and referrals. An agent needs to understand the value of activity. It's all about seeing enough people. If you do that, everything else will fall in place."

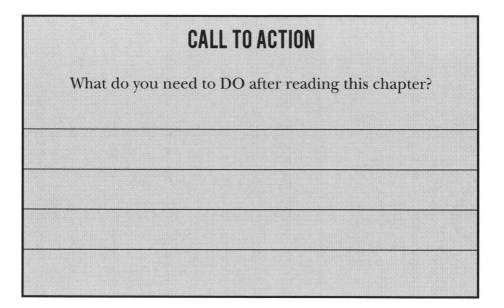

CALL TO ACTION

What do you need to DO after reading this chapter?

Chapter 10

EMBRACING TECHNOLOGY

"Technology isn't going away, so we need to embrace it wisely. However, the most important thing is building mutually beneficial relationships with our customers."
–Terry Brock, technology speaker

Theme:
Are you using cutting-edge technology to be more effective and efficient?

Key Points:
- Investing in the right technology tools
- Acknowledging the technology learning curve
- Valuing personal relationships above technology

When I think about how far we've come with technology over the past couple of centuries, the Pony Express story comes to mind. This innovative transportation service began on April 3, 1860. Mail could be delivered in ten days or less from St. Joseph, Missouri, to Sacramento, California—a 1,966-mile trek using much of the Oregon-California Trail. It was an astounding feat and a hefty investment in those days.

There were 190 relay stations positioned 10–15 miles apart. There were 80 horseback riders, who each carried up to 20 pounds of mail during a 75-mile shift. Some 400 horses were required to keep the animals fresh. Riders, armed only with two revolvers and a knife, were paid $100–$150 per month, a sizable sum in the mid-1800s. The mail was lost once in 650,000 miles of riding.

Despite its popularity and superb track record, the Pony Express ended on October 23, 1861—less than nineteen months after it was launched. What happened? Modern technology made this service obsolete. The Pony Express was replaced by the telegraph. Messages could be received in minutes, not days. What's fascinating is that the Pony Express investors weren't blindsided by the invention of the telegraph.

Samuel Morse completed the first telegraph in 1836, nearly a quarter of a century before the Pony Express began. Morse patented his invention in 1840. He expanded this service in 1846 from New York, New York, to Washington, DC. By 1851, there were more than fifty telegraph companies in the United States. On April 4, 1856, twelve of these companies formed Western Union Telegraph Co., the beginning of unified service. The first transcontinental message was sent by Stephen Field, California chief justice, to President Abraham Lincoln in Washington, DC, on October 23, 1861—the very day the Pony Express ceased to exist.

Moral of the story: Modern technology can make your business obsolete. Or it can turbocharge your agency by enabling you to quote more quickly, handle claims seamlessly, market more inexpensively and track all sorts of activities with the click of a computer mouse. If you've embraced technology, welcome to the twenty-first century. If not, consider the consequences of complacency and be grateful for what technology can do to expand your agency.

Investing In The Right Technology Tools

This chapter subsection isn't focused on providing a comprehensive list of technology tools available in the marketplace. That would take a tome. The intent is to urge you to invest in whatever technology will make your agency more successful and profitable.

"I'm all for technology," said Dave Christy, an agent with three locations in the Spokane, Washington, area. "I helped build a prospecting tool used extensively by the insurance company I represent. However, I don't want my team paying so much attention to technology that they don't get any work done. If it's too cumbersome, it's not going to be productive or efficient. I want technology to assist us, not slow us down. There must be a balance between productivity and suffocation."

Ray Cornprobst, a retired field leader in The Villages, Florida, believes "a specified team member should own the technology duties at an agency. Let this person be the expert. Get this person trained and let him or her educate the rest of the team, including the agent. Obviously, every team member should be reasonably tech savvy, but most of the responsibility should rest on the shoulders of the team technology specialist."

"I think most agents are now seeing the value of technology," says Don Rood Jr., a field leader in Los Angeles, California. "Generally, the only pushback is a lack of confidence or know-how. You have to do business with customers on their terms or you're giving away business to the competition. You have to spend time figuring out how to make technology work for your agency. If customers want to interact through text, email or social media, accept their preferred method of communication. Everything has to be customer-centric."

Acknowledging The Technology Learning Curve

Terry Brock is one of the world's top technology speakers. In 1993, while visiting Terry at his office, I said with the greatest amount of sincerity, "I'll never have a computer!" My perception was that technology was too difficult to master. Besides, I was doing fine without a computer. In retrospect, it's truly embarrassing to tell you about my shortsightedness and naivety.

Thankfully, Terry showed me a few things on his computer and made it look rather simple. I spent $4,000 on a computer and printer the following week. My purchase was overpriced and anti-quated by today's standards, but it was a start. I soon discovered it wasn't so easy to master technology and nearly threw my computer out the window several times in the first six months. Finally, I went to a full-day training class, was able to work with the instructor one-on-one due to mass cancellations and learned more in eight hours than in the previous half year.

Now, all these years later, I'm no technology whiz like my friend Terry. However, it's truly astonishing how much more efficient and effective I am with my growing knowledge of computer science. I've saved hundreds of man-hours and thousands of dollars thanks to modern technology. It's hard to imagine not having email, instant access to documents and the Internet, the ability to view videos and websites and so on. The information age is truly incredible.

Of course, I'm not the only one who has resisted technology. I'm reminded of a seminar in Alabama several years ago. Two veter-an agents approached me at a break. One agent pointed to his friend and said, "This agent has been in the same place for forty-four years." I thought he meant the same office location and com-mended him on such longevity. The agent laughed and corrected me: "No, I mean he hasn't changed a thing at his office in forty-four years!"

A California field leader says: "You're not even in the considera-tion game with the younger generation if you're not into technol-ogy. Your absence is obvious if you're not using social media. Get to know potential customers based on their posted comments. It's better to create an image of being involved in your community. Young people don't want to read about how to keep their home pipes from freezing. They're more interested in knowing how you've helped your customers."

Perhaps you have some longtime team members who haven't em-braced technology. They believe it's something strictly for the younger generation. They refuse to learn and adapt. If so, isn't it in your best interest to urge these people to retire or move on to something else? Why not replace them with more technology-oriented employees?

Scott Foster says: "We're constantly trying to embrace technology and make our work more seamless. We're communicating more with our customers through social media. We're always searching for ways to make things less expensive and more customer friend-ly. These younger team members are into technology and eager to learn more. I remember walking into one team member's office and seeing her with an iPod in one ear and a wireless phone in the other while typing on a keyboard in her lap."

"The good thing about these young agents and team members," says Al Clark, an agent in Arlington, Texas, "is they're motivated, competitive and tech savvy. We old-timers can learn a lot about technology from the younger generation. I'm used to face-to-face meetings with customers, but most of our new business is done by phone, text or email. We haven't met probably 80 percent of our younger customers. The biggest change is definitely in how we gain and write new business."

Valuing Personal Relationships Above Technology

Many agents are frustrated with the so-called millennial generation and its preference for technology over personal relationships.
Transactions are being done on laptops and iPhones, particularly
on auto and home coverage. It's getting more difficult to convince
these twenty-somethings about the importance of visiting an agency to discuss more complex risks.

You can long for the "good old days" and get beat by more tech-
savvy competitors. Or you can do business with prospective customers on their terms and have an opportunity to make the sale.
One thing's certain: you can't develop long-term relationships
with the younger generation if they never become customers.

The blessing of modern technology is greater efficiency and effectiveness. The curse is often a growing reliance on gadgets and a
diminishing affinity for personal relationships. For example, when
you're constantly monitoring your iPhone or laptop in public,
you miss out on interesting conversations with others, including
potential customers. When you send a coworker an email when
your offices are two doors apart, you miss out on a more personal
connection. And when you text a friend, you might have accomplished more with a telephone call.

Cliff Ourso, an agent in Donaldsonville, Louisiana, has embraced
technology at his agency, but he knows firsthand that there's no
substitute for the physical presence of an agent during a disaster.
Many of his customers have suffered extensive property damage
from several hurricanes over the years. They know Cliff and his
team will be on-site to make good on their promises. Technology
can make the claims process smoother and speedier, but it can

never replace a concerned agency team looking customers in the eye and assuring them that they'll make things right.

Purchasing something on Amazon.com isn't the same as buying insurance and financial services. With a few keystrokes, that book or household product is on your doorstep the next day. However, when customers need life insurance, long-term care insurance, investments and estate planning, a personal relationship sure beats calling an 800 number, listening to countless voice prompts, being put on hold for what seems like forever and, if you're fortunate, actually talking to a caring, competent person.

Scott Foster certainly believes there are certain advantages to meeting a customer in person. "You can build a better relationship when you're looking across from each other. It's easier to uncover needs when you can see their reaction to your questions. Emotions are important, particularly when you're discussing financial services. So even if we get new customers via technology, we let them know why it's important to develop a face-to-face relationship and we work hard to make it happen."

"I'm still old school about building personal relationships with our customers," says Todd Jackson, an agent in Anchorage, Alaska. "Fortunately, most Alaskans prefer face-to-face meetings. We invite our customers to meet the team and enjoy some fresh cookies. We try to do about fifteen customer reviews per week because things are always changing in our business. We don't want any surprises when it comes to our customers having the proper protection."

Two really smart men understood that technology is created by people for people so that they can get more done in a timely, cost-effective manner.

Albert Einstein, one of the most intelligent persons who ever lived, remarked, "The human spirit must prevail over technology."

The late Steve Jobs, the innovative co-founder of Apple, maintained: "Technology is nothing. What's important is that you have faith in people...that they're basically good and smart...and if you give them tools, they'll do wonderful things with them."

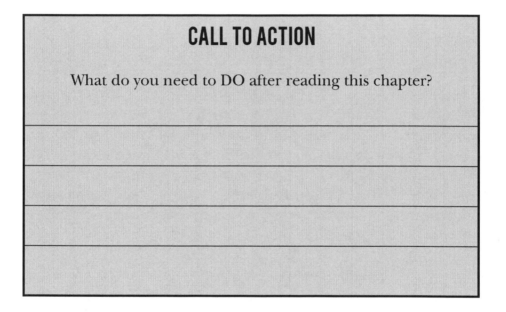

CALL TO ACTION

What do you need to DO after reading this chapter?

TIER 3:
THE TEAM-FOCUSED LEADER

It's about the agency and deliberate delegation

Trusting In Teamwork

Gaining The Talent

Training The Team

Retaining & Sustaining Peak Performers

Attaining A Dream Team

Chapter 11:

TRUSTING IN TEAMWORK

"Each team member is a piece of the puzzle, and each one is needed to complete the picture. No one piece is more important than the other, including the team leader piece."
–Michael L. Miller, *The Infinite Power Of Teams*

Theme:
Are you more of a micromanager or deliberate delegator?

Key Points:
- Ego-driven agent or team-focused agency
- Three teamwork tenets to treasure
- The triumph of team unity

Teamwork isn't optional in the Marine Corps. You learn this immediately at boot camp. Everything is geared toward the success of the platoon, a group of seventy-five recruits under the strict leadership of the drill instructors (DIs). I was in Platoon 295, Second Battalion, Recruit Training Regiment, Parris Island, South Carolina for twelve grueling weeks in late 1964. It was an ordeal that turned immature boys into warrior men, and independent individuals into a collective fighting force.

Now, I realize that you can't operate an insurance agency like a military organization. If you're barking out orders like a marine DI, your team members will probably walk out the door. I was stuck on that island and couldn't leave without suffering severe consequences. But be it a marine unit or an insurance agency, a trustworthy team is necessary to achieve success.

Teamwork is a by-product of great leadership. So, what's your leadership style? Are you a hard-nosed micromanager who squashes the morale and initiative of your team? Or are you a deliberate delegator who entrusts a competent group of people with a myriad of daily activities you could never do by yourself?

In the late 1990s and early 2000s, I had the privilege of delivering a lot of John Maxwell's leadership and teamwork programs. One of the things John would say often is, "If you have to remind the team that you're the leader, you've got an ego problem." **Tip:** Great leaders trust their teams and give them as much credit as possible.

Ego-Driven Agent Or Team-Focused Agency

I get it. You're the undisputed business owner because your signature appears on the agency contract. You're the undisputed business owner because your name is etched in big letters on that sign in front of the agency. You're the undisputed business owner because your money makes it all possible.

Yet how many successful agencies have you seen with a do-it-all leader? You can't grow your book of business without a talented team. **Key question:** Do you want the agency to nose-dive on your ego, or soar on the wings of a dynamic team?

At a National Speakers Association convention years ago, I was fortunate to attend a session led by Zig Ziglar. He was already a legendary speaker and author, but it was Zig's humility that made him special. "Excessive ego is the biggest thing that will kill your career.

Your speaking engagements should always be about the audience, not you." (Note: Zig passed away in 2013.)

Similarly, shouldn't you be focused on your team members and customers, not self-gratification? Check out these dozen contrasts between an ego-driven agent and a team-focused agency:

- Like to get your way **vs.** Love for the agency to stay
- Have an insensitive attitude **vs.** Have a sense of gratitude
- Repress the ideas of others **vs.** Address the ideas of others
- Reject feedback as harmful **vs.** Accept feedback as helpful
- Drive to change everyone else **vs.** Strive to change yourself
- See only personal goals **vs.** Foresee the vision of the agency
- You say, "I can do it all!" **vs.** You ask, "Can I count on y'all?"
- Speak quickly without thinking **vs.** Think quietly before speaking
- Dwell on the weaknesses of others **vs.** Sell the strengths of others
- Tend to whine about problems **vs.** Bend to work toward solutions
- Waste time belaboring others **vs.** Spend time laboring for the agency
- Sad if you don't get the glory **vs.** Glad when the team is the story

In thinking about the agency, how would you characterize it?

- Do you say "my agency" or "our agency"? The former implies that you're the boss and everyone else isn't. The latter shows a "we're all in this together" attitude.
- Do you say "staff" or "team" in referring to your employees? A staff is "a long stick carried in the hand…a rod carried as a symbol of authority." It suggests hierarchy, with an author-

itative figure using force to keep things under control. By contrast, a team is associated with togetherness and focused more on agency accomplishment than on individual achievement, although personal goals are vitally important.

- Do you create the annual business plan by yourself or get the team involved? The only way you're going to get complete buy-in to this plan is if every team member has an ownership stake. The best way to do this is for the plan to be a group endeavor.
- Do you dominate the talking at the weekly agency meetings or do you invite team participation? Heed the words of Dr. Ken Blanchard: "None of us is as smart as all of us."

E. G. Warren, an agent in Gulfport, Mississippi, says: "I tell everyone to check their ego at the door when they come to work each day. I rotate the facilitation of the weekly meeting among our team members. I often let a different team member sit at my desk while conducting these meetings. We're all in this together. I like to ask, 'Who do you want in the foxhole with you?' We can't have real team unity if ego gets in the way."

Bill Thorp, an agent in Grants Pass, Oregon, says: "We're nothing without the team. Every team member is important. You have to love on them all the time. I like to take mongrels and turn them into thoroughbreds. So often the people you think will be your best team members turn out not to be. I want loyalty, loyalty, loyalty. I want hard workers. I want people who want to be self-employed without the responsibility."

I often have agents participate in a skit entitled "Colors." Based on an American Indian legend, it's designed to show how each team member plays an important part in the overall agency success. I ask the participants to passionately act out their part of the skit.

It usually produces a humorous, highly effective demonstration about the need for teamwork:

Once upon a time the colors of the world started to quarrel. All claimed they were the best, the most important, the most useful, the favorite.

GREEN *said: "Clearly, I am the most important. I am the sign of life. I was chosen for grass, trees and leaves. Without me, all animals would die. Look over the countryside and you'll see that I am in the majority."*

BLUE *interrupted: "You only think about the earth, but consider the sky and sea. It's water that is the basis of life and is drawn up by the clouds from the deep blue sea. The sky gives space, peace and serenity. Without me, all of you would be nothing."*

YELLOW *chuckled: "You all are so serious. I bring laughter, gaiety and warmth into the world. The sun is yellow, the moon is yellow and the stars are yellow. Every time you look at a sunflower, the world starts to smile. Without me, there would be no fun."*

ORANGE *started next to blow its horn: "I am the color of health and strength. I may be scarce, but I am precious, for I serve the needs of human life. I carry the most vitamins. Think of carrots, pumpkins, oranges and mangos. I don't hang around all the time, but when I fill the sky at sunset or sunrise, my beauty is so striking that no one gives another thought to any of you."*

RED *could stand it no longer and shouted: "I am the ruler of all. I am blood—life's blood. I am the color of danger and bravery. I am willing to fight for a cause. Without me, the earth would be as empty as the moon. I am the color of passion, love, the red rose, poinsettia and poppy."*

PURPLE rose to its full height, speaking with great pomp. "I am the color of royalty and power. Kings, chiefs and bishops have always chosen me, for I am the sign of authority and wisdom. People don't question me. They listen and obey."

Finally, INDIGO spoke, much more quietly than all the others, but with just as much determination. "Think of me. I am the color of silence. I'm hardly noticed, but without me you all become superficial. I represent thought, reflection, twilight and deep water. You need me for balance and contrast, for prayer and inner peace."

And so the colors went on boasting, each convinced of his or her superiority. The quarreling became louder and louder. Suddenly, there was a startling flash of bright lightning. Thunder rolled and boomed. Rain poured down relentlessly. The colors crouched in fear, drawing closer to each other for comfort.

In the midst of the clamor, the rain began to speak: "You colors are so foolish. Why are you fighting among yourselves and trying to dominate the rest? Don't you know you were made for a special purpose, unique and different? Join hands with one another and come to me."

Doing as they were told, the colors united and joined hands. The rain continued: "From now on, when it rains, each of you will stretch across the sky in a great hue of color as a reminder that you can all live in peace. The rainbow is a sign of hope for tomorrow."

And so, whenever a good rain bathes the world and a rainbow appears in the sky, let us remember to appreciate one another.

Why not try this skit with your team? If you only have three or four people, they'll have to play several parts, but it's doable. Follow these instructions:

1. Cut out each of the skit paragraphs before your meeting, number them 1–12 and keep them in the proper order.
2. Ask your team members to line up in a semicircle at the front of the room.
3. Hand a strip of paper to each team member, starting with the person on the far left (number 1) and proceeding to the person on the far right (number 12).
4. Ask everyone to read *silently* what you've just handed out.
5. Urge all participants to act out what they're about to read aloud, paying special attention to voice inflections, gestures, facial expressions, demonstrative behavior and so on.
6. Have each team member read aloud his or her paragraph(s), starting with the person on the far left and proceeding to the far right.

If this exercise is done correctly and enthusiastically, you'll make a memorable point about trusting in teamwork.

Three Teamwork Tenets To Treasure

I learned many valuable lessons about teamwork as a marine sergeant. The corps is a diverse group of individuals—men and women from all races, cultures, backgrounds, religions, geographic areas and personal interests. Yet there's an *esprit de corps* or "common spirit" that creates "enthusiasm, devotion and a strong regard for the honor of the group." It's what makes the Marine Corps a unique team.

I suspect your agency is also comprised of many different people. As the leader, you must be able to balance the concepts of independence, dependence and interdependence in order for your agency to run smoothly. Let's examine each component by looking at the similarities between the recruitment of a marine and an agency team member:

Independence—The Marine Corps is seeking tough-minded, strong-willed recruits who are willing to sacrifice personal glory for the sake of the team. In the civilian world, perhaps no other small business owner is more independent than an insurance agent. Therefore, doesn't it make sense to recruit independent self-starters to help you build your business? Shouldn't you hire highly confident people who possess an entrepreneurial mind-set and a competitive spirit?

"Independence" may sound anti-teamwork and counterintuitive, but nothing could be farther from the truth. While independent people tend to be achievement oriented, they also know that individual success is linked closely to the collective support of the team. Remember: a chain is only as strong as its weakest link. Why would you retain team members who aren't pulling their share of the agency load?

Dependence—Marines are dependent upon their fellow leathernecks to be victorious in warfare. It's no different on the business battlefield. The true test of your leadership skills is molding a group of independent team members into a cohesive unit. Think of your agency team as the rainbow you've just read about—many different colors that come together to produce a beautiful sight. When assembled properly, a dream team can take your agency to new heights of productivity, profitability and fulfillment.

I once talked to an agent who'd fired his entire team because he was frustrated with their inept performance. He went from dependent to truly independent overnight. More than likely, his production plummeted and his stress skyrocketed. If you can't depend on your team, how will you ever grow your agency?

Interdependence—For the Marine Corps to prevail in battle, it's often necessary to cooperate closely with the navy, army and air force. To win at your agency, you have to rely on the interdependence of numerous business partners (internal and external) who provide a variety of support services. For example, you depend on the home office to create products, underwrite and issue policies, pay commissions, advertise, handle claims, take care of legal matters, deal with the government, represent the profession and engage in many other activities you probably don't have the skills, resources or time to do.

Reach out to these people and cultivate long-term relationships. They may not be on your payroll, but these partners are generating countless dividends to your agency. Instead of making their jobs harder by complaining and criticizing, let them know how much you appreciate their efforts to make your agency more successful. It's a win-win for everyone.

The Triumph Of Team Unity

You can learn a lot about teamwork from the marines. First, it takes a unified team to win big. Second, healthy teams provide a support system that makes achievement more satisfying. Third, you can't develop your leadership skills without a team.

It was thrilling to graduate from boot camp and be called a marine for the first time. We were a part of something much grander than individualism. We were carrying on the "esprit de corps" tradition that's helped keep America free since 1775. "The few, the proud, the Marines" wasn't just a slogan anymore. Our DIs had molded seventy-five raw civilians into a team of leathernecks who felt honored to serve their nation. It was truly a triumph of team unity.

Similarly, if you build a competent team, you're positioning your agency to vie for the lion's share of the marketplace while helping more customers minimize their risks and maximize their dreams. Gradually, small agency staffs are going the way of the typewriter, rotary telephone and mimeograph machine. Proactive agents are building bigger, more knowledgeable teams, entering the battle and fighting to win.

Micromanaging destroys confidence and initiative. If you don't trust your team members to do their jobs, why did you hire them? Sure, it takes time to train and trust team members, but if the right talent is on board, the last thing good people want is you constantly looking over their shoulders. When team members make mistakes, do you castigate them or provide teaching moments to help them learn, move on and improve?

Speaker Patricia Fripp says, "There's no point doing well that which you shouldn't be doing at all." Great agents are deliberate delegators. It's about trusting a team of highly skilled people to do what you can't do alone. It allows you to spend more time leading the team instead of managing activities. The result is higher morale, greater productivity and better team longevity.

Bill Epperly spent twenty-five years as an agent and ten years in leadership for a major insurance company. The author of *Stoneage Marketing*, Bill says: "The number one job of a leader is to hire and train. Thriving is a matter of putting together and managing the best team possible. As a leader, your job is to create the culture, climate and conditions for the team to be effective."

Bill adds: "I still see too many agents who are better technicians than they are team leaders. They're spending too much time on sales instead of leading a team of sales and service specialists. They're woefully understaffed. They're coasting primarily on renewals. As a result, the agency is experiencing lower productivity, revenues and profits." He urges agents to follow these three principles in building a high-performing, unified team:

Engagement—If an agent doesn't involve the team members in the decision-making process, they won't feel empowered or have a strong sense of ownership. Leadership expert John Maxwell says, "He that thinks he leads and has no one following him only takes a walk."

Explanation—Each team member must understand his or her unique role in the overall success of the agency. Knowledge leads to confidence, and confidence produces peak performance provided you have a generous reward system in place.

Expectation—As the leader, you must cast the vision and the team must have the proper goals in place to get the agency to its desired destination. Most importantly, you must hold each team member accountable for his or her successes and failures.

Christine Bailey, an agent in Moss Bluff, Louisiana, says: "My job IS the team. I want each team member to reach the next level and maximize his or her potential. About once a quarter, I like to ask the team if there's anything we need to streamline or tweak. I especially like to get the perspective of new team members. I treat my team with respect. I value their ideas and opinions. We have a good working environment because I don't allow any drama."

Nothing destroys team unity more than conflict, which is defined as "a mental struggle resulting from incompatible or opposing needs." Here are some proven ways to minimize conflict:

- Consider your motives before opening mouth and inserting foot.
- Explore other alternatives besides "we've always done it this way."
- Grasp the long-term consequences of a short-term crisis to put things in perspective.
- Look for opportunities in every obstacle when dealing with people.
- Respect the opinions of others even if you disagree with them.
- Seek common ground instead of dwelling on the differences.
- Know the difference between unrealistic expectations and realistic execution.
- Be a little vulnerable and show a lot of humility.
- Realize that it's more important to make it work than to win at all costs.
- Spend more time mentoring and less time manipulating.

Scott Foster's agency has certain rules to minimize conflict and maximize team unity. For example, a certain number of team members must always be on-site during working hours. When a team member decided to get married during the week to save money, most of the team wanted to attend this special event.

Scott called in the team member who was getting married and reminded her of the rule about having a certain number of people on-site during working hours. Scott asked her to get with the team and work out who'd be attending the wedding and who wouldn't.

Lesson learned: Great leaders lighten their load by teaching problem-solving skills to their team members.

CALL TO ACTION

What do you need to DO after reading this chapter?

Chapter 12:

GAINING THE TALENT

"The most important part of your agency is the people that work for you providing sales and service to customers. As a result, you want to hire the very best people you can find."
–Al Clark, *Al Clark's Multi-Million Dollar Formula 4 Success*

Theme:
Are you offering joyless jobs or challenging careers to prospective team members?

Key Points:
- Recruiting the right people
- Placing the right people in the right positions
- Nurturing team chemistry

Coach John Wooden led UCLA to an unprecedented ten NCAA men's basketball championships, including seven straight. He was a great coach who attracted great talent. In his book *Wooden On Leadership*, the late coach says: "You need talent on your team to prevail in the competitive arena. However, many leaders don't know how to win even when they have great talent in their organization. With all levels of talent, my goal was...to get the most out of what we had."

In thinking about your agency, are you attracting the very best people you can find? Moreover, are you getting the most out of each team member? How you answer these key questions is connected closely to your leadership skills.

Many agents say they were recruited to be salespeople, not leaders. Alas, that was then, and this is now. If you aren't willing to be the CEO of your small business, focusing more on recruiting and training talent and less on selling and servicing, how will you ever attract the best people to perform the sales and service activities necessary to grow your agency?

When you went into agency, you probably viewed it as exciting career, not a mundane job. With that in mind, what's the difference between a joyless job and a challenging career? Here are ten contrasts to consider when assembling the best team possible:

- A job is something you *have* to go to; a career is something you *want* to go to most every day.
- A job is something you often find boring; a career is something you find exciting and challenging most every day.
- A job is something that provides a livelihood; a career is something that will be a vital part of your legacy.
- A job is something you call work; a career is something that's fun most of the time.
- A job is something you usually can't wait to leave at the end of the day; a career is something you usually look forward to the next day.
- A job is something you yearn to retire from; a career is something that often makes retiring difficult to do.
- A job is something you fuss about frequently; a career is something you find fulfilling most of the time.
- A job is something you may leave because you're unhappy; a career is something you stay with because it's your life's passion.

- A job is something that often feels like an unwanted obligation; a career is something that feels like a wanted responsibility.
- A job is something you wouldn't wish on someone else; a career is something you encourage others to consider.

This raises the question: Are you offering joyless jobs or challenging careers to the people who are seeking employment at your agency? Your response says a lot about the state of your agency and the type of talent you have—or would like to have.

Pat Healey, an agent in Lake Oswego, Oregon, and author of *Finding Joy In Your Job,* makes a great observation: "Choose to find joy. Stop putting the onus of the blame on the qualities your job lacks, and start focusing on the happiness that each day brings. When you accept the aspects of your career that you can control—your attitude, spirit and joy—you'll see life in a whole new way." To learn more about Pat's services, go to www.bethebestboss.com.

Recruiting The Right People

In a survey of almost two hundred agents, I asked, "What's your biggest agency challenge?" Overwhelmingly, the top challenge was "finding and keeping a reliable team." I heard countless stories about nightmare agency teams. I was told how frustrating it is to gain and retain good people. **Fact:** To get the right people, you have to be the right leader. If you're experiencing high turnover, the common denominator is YOU, the leader.

Of course, you can do all the right things in recruiting team members, but nothing is foolproof. You're going to lose some people no matter how well you lead. There's no guaranteed way to know what type of people you've hired until they're on board. However, if you hire enough unproductive people, or you lose a lot of productive team members due to your poor leadership skills, it will be an expensive, exasperating experience.

Terri Phillips, a contact center training manager with a major insurance company, says: "An investment of $150 is required to test a prospective team member, but the cost of an undesirable hiring decision is $50,000. If you don't get the right people in the right positions doing the right things, you spend your days feeling like you're pushing frogs in a wheelbarrow. People want to succeed, so set them up for success. If you have a person with no desire to succeed, let that frog jump!"

Andy Stanley, the senior pastor of North Point Ministries in Alpharetta, Georgia, says: "Recruit doers, not thinkers. It's much easier to educate a doer than it is to activate a thinker. You want to have a work group, not a think tank. Put people where they can make their greatest contributions because [your] organization is at its best when team members are doing what they do best."

In recruiting and interviewing prospective team members, you might want to remind them of the following advantages of an agency career:

- The *opportunity* to work in a close-knit, caring small business environment
- The *availability* of a major insurance company's vast resources
- The *possibility* of earning unlimited income without ever asking for a raise
- The *nobility* of serving customers at a time when their needs are the greatest
- The *accessibility* of an agency support team dedicated to your personal growth and professional development

- The *probability* of a long-term career in a virtually recession-proof profession
- The *flexibility* of balancing the work you do with the life you lead

Christine Bailey, an agent in Moss Bluff, Louisiana, says this about hiring. "When we bring on new people, it's for a ninety-day trial period. This is done for the new person and me. It gives both of us an out if things don't go well. I want to see if someone can produce and be a team player. I'm constantly evaluating. I don't hesitate to help a person find a different occupation. I want career team members, not paycheck people. Our business is so much bigger than that."

Christine continues: "I don't like an office full of high-powered, A-type sales people. I'm looking for 'Steady Eddie' producers, not people who are up and down. As a result, my compensation plan is about 70 percent base salary and 30 percent commissions/bonuses. This encourages reliable, across-the-board production month after month while minimizing burnout. The proof's in the numbers."

A more aggressive approach is taken by Trey Rhodes, an agent with locations in Newnan and Carrollton, Georgia. "In recruiting new team members, we use Wonderlic, a cognitive ability test to assess aptitude for learning and problem solving. If they hit a certain score (at least 23 for salespeople), I interview them. I set expectations at the outset because if you're not producing early on, my people will force you out."

Trey goes on: "My ten salespeople all want to be agents one day. I expect them to work from eight in the morning to eight at night for the first six months. In addition to working hard, they must be coachable. I pay them a monthly salary of $1,000, plus commissions and bonuses. We run at a high level, so not everyone makes it here. I tried a softer approach early on and found it didn't work."

Al Clark, an agent in Arlington, Texas, says: "It takes a more talented person to be a team member than when I started in 1979. The agencies of the future will be a lot bigger because we keep adding more products. It's hard for small teams to keep up with everything. We've always tried to hire career people, train them well and give them a lot of authority and responsibility in pursuing our agency goals."

Placing The Right People In The Right Positions

In my junior and senior years at East Atlanta High School, I took an aptitude test to determine my natural talents. The mechanical, scientific, artistic, outdoor and social service sections were pathetically low. The clerical, literary, persuasive, musical and computational sections were extremely high. In reviewing these tests more than a half century later, they've proved to be quite accurate.

To this day, I can't fix anything. I'm not curious about science. I can't even draw a fly. I've never been a fisherman, a hunter or anything like that. Having grown up with parents who were Salvation Army officers, I'm all for social service but, frankly, it's not my strongest aptitude.

On the other hand, I've always been good at organization and administration. I'm an avid reader. I've used persuasive skills throughout my career. I love music. The one exception is my computational score, which was a fluke. The only course I failed in high school was algebra. Needless to say, I never made it to geometry, calculus and trigonometry.

Key point: People tend to excel in the areas where they're naturally gifted. You put salespeople in service positions and they'll probably be miserable. You put service people in sales positions and they'll probably be unhappy. You put disorganized people in administrative positions and they'll probably be frustrated. Getting the right people in the right positions is one of the most important things you can do as an agency leader.

A popular testing tool for getting the right people in the right positions is Kolbe. Rather than measure IQ or personality, this test will help you do the following:

- Identify the *instinctive style of behavior* of each team member
- Allow individuals to perform better by playing to their strengths
- Enable teams to perform better by understanding the natural instincts of each team member
- Improve relationships through greater respect for each team member's natural style
- Stop team members from forcing others to do things "their way"
- Enhance the decision-making and problem-solving abilities of each team member

Founder Kathy Kolbe maintains, "When people are free to act according to their own natural instincts—and respect those of others—wonderful things begin to happen."

Todd Jackson, an agent in Anchorage, Alaska, likes the Gallup StrengthFinders 2.0 online aptitude assessment. "It's a tool to help a person identify what they do best. Some thirty-six core talents are measured. No one is good at everything, but everyone is good at something. We've found if we get the right people in the right positions, we're better collectively."

Brooks Baltich, an agent in Richmond, Virginia, speaks often on screening, interviewing and hiring team members. "Sometimes you have to make an exception to the rules and take a risk. I remember interviewing a guy in his sixties. He was overweight and weird looking. I gave him a test to measure sales aptitude and he failed. In reviewing his resume, I noticed that he had ten years of telemarketing experience. I probably shouldn't have hired him but did anyway. He led our zone in production that year!"

"I try to help my agents define their organizational structure," says Johanna Kelly, a field leader in Binghamton, New York. "They must know the exact positions they're hiring for. Every agency position should be so well defined that each team member can name the top three responsibilities of every other team member."

Johanna continues: "Agents should hire really intelligent people who can develop quickly. A lot of agents say it takes a long time to train team members. However, if you hire the right people, there's no reason why they can't be licensed and trained in eight weeks. With so many documented learning paths available today, including virtual training, it has never been easier to recruit, hire and lead an agency team."

Ray Cornprobst, a retired field leader in The Villages, Florida, says: "Agents should always be recruiting. Get your team members to help you with this effort. Have them post any available job opportunities on social networking sites, and then follow up on all responses. Great people tend to hang out with great people."

P. J. Johnson, an agent in North Charleston, South Carolina, uses Career Plug, a company that posts positions and generates a lot of team member applicants. "I have every team member interview a prospective new associate. Potential new hires have to spend four hours with my service person to get a feel for what we do."

P. J. continues: "I also give them a birthday list and have them make calls for an hour to see how many appointments they can make. I can see if they're good on the phone. Generally, I know if someone is going to make it in the first four weeks. We want to be known as a professional agency, not a sweat shop."

Nurturing Team Chemistry

"There's nothing more important on a team than chemistry," maintains Bill Kolb, an agent in Pryor, Oklahoma. "I'll take chemistry over talent and test scores every time. I tell my team we're not working against each other. We're working against everyone else because there's a lot of competition out there. The last thing we need on a team is conflict. That's why I like for my team members to interview prospective new employees. Yes, I have the final say, but I want to make sure my team is comfortable with new hires."

Bill tells an interesting story about a time when two of his team members were at odds. "One of them burst into my office ranting about the other team member. She wanted to know what I was going to do about this situation. I told her I'd talk with the other team member that day. Then, I would sleep on it that night and fire one of them the following day. The next day the adamant team member apologized to her workmate!"

Christine Bailey, an agent in Moss Bluff, Louisiana, takes this approach: "We do a lot of things together. We celebrated with a trip to New Orleans. We went on a cruise. We had a crawfish boil. We had a Super Bowl party at the office. We participated in a cancer fund-raiser called 'Relay For Life.' These activities foster bonding and team chemistry."

If you're struggling with team harmony, most likely it's due to the following circumstances:

Negativism—The old adage of "one bad apple spoils the whole barrel" is especially true in a small team environment. When cynicism is prevalent, it permeates the workplace. It leads to lower morale, diminished productivity and increased tension and turmoil. It's best to lose the bad attitude and resist the urge to make everyone else miserable.

Selfishness—Howard Ferguson says in *The Edge*: "The team player knows the team comes first. It doesn't matter who gets the credit as long as the job gets done. If the job gets done, the credit will come." Perhaps nothing destroys team chemistry more than excessive ego.

Jealousy—No team member should be envious of another associate's success. Lift each other up when things go well; be there for each other when times are tough. Healthy competition is good for the team and agency. If jealousy is eating away at your team chemistry, get rid of this insidious cancer.

Drama—Intense emotional conflict should be left to the television soap operas because it has no place in your agency. It draws unnecessary attention to a particular team member and creates unneeded stress for everyone else. Such behavior is selfish and immature, and a deterrent to team unity. Make drama a "no tolerance" imperative.

Gossip—Do you want "a person who habitually reveals personal or sensational facts about others" working in your agency? Spreading rumors about team members not only is a waste of valuable time, but it also sabotages trust and team unity. What was it your mother used to say? "If you can't say something good about someone, don't say anything."

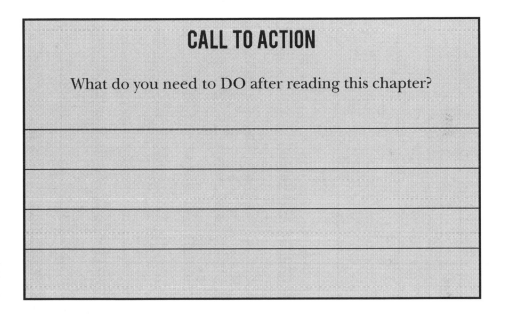

CALL TO ACTION

What do you need to DO after reading this chapter?

Chapter 13:
TRAINING THE TEAM

"What's worse than training your workers and losing them to other organizations? You don't train them and they stay!"
–Zig Ziglar

Theme:
Do you have a specific plan of personal growth and professional development for every team member, agent included?

Key Points:
- Communicating agency culture
- Concentrating on product knowledge and sales skills
- Cultivating an unquenchable thirst for lifelong learning

I left journalism for the sales profession in 1970. Even though I had absolutely no sales experience, it was an economic move due to the difficulty of subsisting on a $400 gross monthly income as an Associated Press staff writer. Somehow, I did well in my first year of sales despite minimal guidance. What I lacked in product knowledge and sales training, I made up for with people skills and persistence.

The following year, it was my good fortune to do business with Jim Porterfield of Sales Training, Inc. (STI). Jim convinced me to enroll in STI's five-month sales training course. Yes, my sales and income improved dramatically during this training, but the best thing about this experience is that it taught me the value of ongoing learning.

All these years later, I'm surrounded by the tools of my trade. I've collected hundreds of books, seminar handouts, CDs and videos that have taught me about sales, leadership, teamwork, communication, work/life balance, spiritual matters and more. If you haven't done so already, why not establish an agency library for the personal growth and professional development of you and your team?

Unfortunately, I've seen a lot of agents and team members who have no specific growth plan. This is unfortunate. They go through their careers aimlessly. They miss out on the excitement of continuing education. They wonder why they don't reach their full potential.

Think about it. Would you drive from New York to Florida without planning your route? If so, be prepared for a longer, more expensive journey. In planning your life and livelihood, doesn't it make infinitely more sense to map out where you're going and how you plan to get there?

Communicating Agency Culture

There are three primary components of agency culture that require constant communication:

Purpose—Why does the agency do what it does? Do you have an agency purpose statement? (See chapter 2)

Vision—Where is the agency going over the next five years and beyond? Do you have an agency vision statement? (See chapter 4)

Values—What does the agency believe in and stand for? Do you have an agency values statement? (See chapter 5)

In *Above The Board: How Ethical CEOs Create Honest Corporations*, Patrizia Porrini, Lorene Hiris and Gina Poncini state: "The ethical climate of an organization is fundamental in guiding employee behavior, and such a climate depends on leadership and concrete initiatives that encourage continuous adherence to a company's core values."

The authors define company culture as "the customary beliefs, social forms and material traits of a group...the set of shared attitudes, values and practices that characterize a company."

A big part of agency culture is created through training and clear communication. Avoid certain communication barriers and model certain communication boosters. A barrier is "an obstacle that impedes or separates; something that blocks an intended message." It's difficult, if not impossible, to create a congruent agency culture without clear communication.

Here are some common **communication barriers**:

- Mishandling conflicts
- Blowing problems out of proportion
- Giving feedback improperly
- Disseminating misinformation
- Assuming everyone knows what you know
- "Planning" everything spontaneously
- Being too judgmental before you have all the facts
- Displaying adverse body language
- Being too insensitive or offensive (of course, this can be taken to the extreme)
- Failing to dole out lots of appreciation and recognition

By contrast, a booster is "a device that increases effectiveness; something that provides strong support." Here are some practical **communication boosters**:

- Think before speaking.
- Go beyond passive hearing to active listening.
- Have more questions than answers.
- Do more relating than ranting.
- Focus more on solutions than problems.
- Strive to see the other person's point of view.
- Value the long-term relationship more than the short-term situation.
- Respect the space of others.
- Forgive easily and ask for forgiveness.
- Smile!

Scott Garvey, an agent in Baltimore, Maryland, does a superb job of communicating his agency culture. New team members are given a little booklet entitled *Scott Garvey's Playbook*. Besides the agency purpose statement found in chapter 2, it also includes the agency's values statement:

- We are accountable in all we do.
- We embrace change to sharpen our competitive edge.
- We develop innovative systems and use them.
- We empower a positive and energetic environment.
- We communicate openly and honestly using Safe Space ©. (This is a tool for creating a culture in which all team members can speak freely about all things.)
- We believe in ongoing training, coaching and mentoring to refine our skills.
- We are a positive force in our community.
- We perform as a team with a champion mind-set.

- We are fiscally healthy.
- We have FUN!

Concentrating On Product Knowledge And Sales Skills

Scott Foster does three types of training every week at his agency. He does training for his service people on Tuesday, 8:00–9:00 a.m. He does sales training on Wednesday, 7:00–9:00 a.m. He holds team meetings on Thursday, 8:00–9:00 a.m.

In addition, Scott calls periodic ten-minute huddles with his team to see if "we're on track with our goals and where we are as an agency. I probably go overboard with training, but you have to communicate constantly to make sure the team is headed in the right direction."

One of the best ways to incorporate product knowledge with sales skills is to make role-playing a weekly activity at your agency. Scott and financial services representative Mark King spend a lot of time role-playing with the team. It's an ideal way for team members to receive valuable feedback about the way they interact with customers, how they identify needs and how they present various products as solutions to these needs.

Trey Rhodes, a Scott Foster protégé and an agent with locations in Newnan and Carrollton, Georgia, says: "We use something called the 'Training Wheel' with our salespeople. It works this way: (1) Tell them. (2) Show them. (3) Watch them. (4) Have them teach others. I expect my salespeople to be teaching newer salespeople early on because the best way to learn something is to teach it. We also do a lot of role-playing, which is a real confidence builder."

Stan Simmons, an agent in Lawrenceburg, Kentucky, is also a training advocate. "I just taught 'client-centered selling' to the team. I have every team member attend at least one boot camp offered by the company I represent. I have my field leader sit in on joint appointments for customer reviews, which has helped take us to the next level. I have outside mentoring relationships. Without knowledge, confidence suffers—and when confidence suffers, sales suffer!"

"I quit teaching people skills a long time ago," says Bill Kolb, an agent in Pryor, Oklahoma. "I can help you with core skills like product knowledge and sales training, but if someone isn't good with people, I can't teach that. I want a team member, not a project. If you can't sell yourself to me during the hiring process, there's a good chance I've got a project. It's like teaching someone how to run a 4.3 in the forty-meter dash. You either have God-given speed or you don't."

Bill adds: "Most agents spend 90 percent of their time on sales and service, and only 10 percent on product knowledge. If there's an Achilles heel in any agency, it's product knowledge. If team members can't educate customers on our products, how can we expect customers to believe in these products, much less buy them? If you aren't getting production out of your team members, it's generally because they don't know how to or they don't want to. Both will cost you a lot of money."

"There's no money better spent at an agency than that spent on developing your people," maintains Ray Cornprobst, a retired field leader in The Villages, Florida. "It's a better investment than the stock market. Sometimes you don't need more team members; you just need to train the ones you already have. Agents need to think about investing in their businesses—and it starts with training their teams."

Cultivating An Unquenchable Thirst For Lifelong Learning

If you believe every team member, agent included, should have a specific plan for his or her personal growth and professional development, here are seven suggested learning opportunities ranging from daily to ongoing:

Read from a good book at least fifteen minutes *daily*. The late Charlie "Tremendous" Jones said in *Life Is Tremendous*, "You'll be the same in five years as you are today except for the people you meet and the books you read." If you can't read at least fifteen minutes each day, could you be too busy? Use the best of what you read for inspirational moments at your team meetings.

Listen to educational/inspirational CDs *weekly*. I like the term "rolling university." It's a good way to make the most of your time in the car and much safer than reading while driving! Audio learning is also a good alternative if you don't like to read. Consider subscribing to a CD-of-the-month club and adding these resources to your agency library.

Learn a new product *monthly*. The late Earl Nightingale believed you could become an expert on a topic by studying one hour a day for a year. **Recommendation:** Why not have every team member study a different product every month for a year? Instead of an hour each day, make a commitment to study a product for just one hour each week. In one year, that's fifty-two hours of product knowledge for each team member.

Attend a how-to seminar *quarterly*. This can be an internal program on product knowledge, service procedures, underwriting changes, technology updates and so on. Or it can be an external training opportunity dealing with leadership, teamwork, communication and more. Perhaps nothing is more informative, inspirational and interactive than a live presentation given by a polished seminar leader. Take ample notes, but focus on three ideas that you can implement right away.

Participate in a study group *semiannually.* By tapping into the wisdom of your peers, you'll shorten your learning curve and accelerate your growth. Make sure these off-site meetings are well-planned to get the maximum return on your time, money and energy.

Write a review *annually.* I had a bad year in 1973. I sat down with a legal pad and pen in late December and wrote about that frustrating year. I've continued this cathartic practice ever since because it (1) teaches me to be thankful for my many blessings regardless of how a year unfolds, (2) puts any struggles from previous years in a "this, too, shall pass" perspective, and (3) challenges me to look forward to the coming year with hope.

Be in *ongoing* **mentoring relationships.** Good mentors see you for what you can become, not for what you are. Therefore, become a connoisseur of caring mentors. You'll learn from these veterans and in the process, you might teach them something as well.

Of all these suggested learning opportunities, perhaps study clubs are the most valuable to top agents. When you have a group of high achievers in the same room, their collective experiences will cover most every situation you'll face in agency leadership. You'll learn a lot while developing a special camaraderie with a group of peers who care about you and your business.

Napoleon Hill, author of the best seller *Think & Grow Rich,* was a pioneer of study clubs or "master mind" groups: "The 'Master Mind' may be defined as coordination of knowledge and effort, in a spirit of harmony, between two or more people, for the attainment of a definite purpose. A group of brains coordinated (or connected) in a spirit of harmony will provide more thought-energy than a single brain, just as a group of electric batteries will provide more energy than a single battery."

Early in my speaking career, I brought a draft of a marketing brochure to my study club meeting. Another speaker reviewed this brochure with two magic markers and handed it back to me, saying: "Dick, you'll notice a lot of yellow markings and very few orange markings. The yellow refers to your credentials; the orange is about what you can do for your prospective customers. You might want to rewrite this brochure. Make about 90 percent of it on what you can do to help organizations [benefits], and the rest on your credentials [bio]."

It proved to be sound advice. My brochure was a huge marketing success. It taught me three valuable lessons: (1) Seek out the perspective of other people. (2) Reap the wisdom of collective minds. (3) Act on what you learn.

A good example is Scott Foster's life insurance study group. Most of these members are Top of the Table agents—the best of the best in MDRT. Scott has never finished out of the top ten agents in life production for the company he represents. He's a lifetime MDRT member. Yet with all of his success, Scott is the lowest producer in this study group. **Lesson learned:** There's enormous value in hanging around people who are more successful than you.

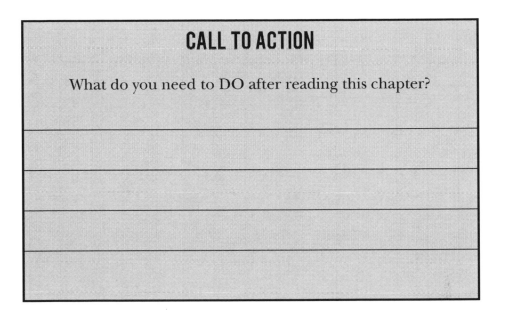

CALL TO ACTION

What do you need to DO after reading this chapter?

Chapter 14

RETAINING & SUSTAINING PEAK PERFORMERS

"The greatest challenge of every business [is] attracting the best people available and retaining them. Creating a company full of rising stars differentiates companies and sustains success."
–Susan Bixler, CEO, Bixler Consulting Group

Theme:
Are you compensating your team members for mediocre or exceptional production?

Key Points:
* Empowering team members with proper feedback
* Recognizing and rewarding team members with the right incentives
* Fostering team loyalty and minimizing turnover

The late Dr. Michael Guido, founder of the Guido Evangelistic Association (GEA) in Metter, Georgia, was a remarkable people person. Judy and I were blessed to call Michael our friend and mentor for twenty years. He passed away on February 21, 2009, at ninety-four. We were among the more than 1,500 people who attended his funeral on a cold, windy and rainy day in southeastern Georgia. We miss those eight-hour round-trip drives to spend time with the most holy, honorable and humble person we've ever known.

Michael had an uncanny ability to make us feel like we were the two most important people in the world. He always wanted to know what was going on in our lives. He was a wonderful listener. He was quick to praise and encourage. We have more than 150 of Michael's uplifting letters, notes and cards in a binder as a special memorial to this great leader.

Michael and Audrey Guido were exceptional employers as well. They had a team of thirteen loyal employees dedicated to GEA's work in sharing the Gospel message primarily through devotional booklets, radio spots and short television messages. And even though GEA—now led by Michael's brother Larry—is totally dependent upon contributions for its financial support, Michael never asked for money. He truly practiced what he preached about faith, always praying devotedly and giving credit to God.

Now, as you think about your agency, there's a lot you can learn about retaining and sustaining peak performers from Dr. Guido's authentic example:

- Be genuinely interested in people.
- Be in the moment.
- Be a good listener.
- Be an encourager.
- Be humble.
- Be honorable.
- Be real.
- Be a person of faith.

Empowering Team Members With Proper Feedback

When I was discharged from the Marine Corps in 1968, I worked for a year as a staff writer for the Associated Press (AP). Having secured this job while the writers and teletype operators were on strike, I never joined their union. My mail slot was filled with nasty notes the entire year. I'd always trash these unsigned messages and look eagerly for a letter from Lamar Matthews, my editor. Mr. Matthews took the time to assess my work from the prior evening via a typewritten letter. He used a special three-part formula:

First, Mr. Matthews praised what I'd done right, which was often a stretch in the early weeks. Nevertheless, he'd find something positive about my work and tell me why he liked it. "Young man, I loved your lead paragraph on the Georgia–Georgia Tech basketball game and here's why." Naturally, his positive praise got my attention.

Second, Mr. Matthews offered "suggestions" for my improvement. This usually took up most of the letter. For instance, Mr. Matthews would cite a particular section of the AP stylebook to support why one word should be used instead of another. Because of his caring approach, I worked hard to get better and please my editor.

Third, Mr. Matthews closed his letters with hope and encouragement. "Son, if you just keep improving, you're going to be one of our best writers ever." In a work environment that was hostile due to my refusal to join the union of my coworkers, this optimistic reinforcement was a welcome ray of sunshine—and a stellar example of how to give proper feedback.

Near the end of my stint at the AP, Mr. Matthews rewarded my improvement with a choice assignment—one that probably should have gone to a veteran writer. I covered the first Naismith award banquet in Atlanta, Georgia. Lew Alcindor of UCLA was the best college basketball player in 1969. One of my prized possessions is a photo of me and Lew—aka Kareem Abdul-Jabbar—and the original teletype story that went out to newspapers across America.

After I told the AP story a few years ago, Tom Pickett sent me a glowing testimonial letter. Tom referred to Mr. Matthews's feedback formula as the "sandwich technique." Tom said my AP editor put the bad news (the meat of how I could improve) between the good news (the bread of what I did right coupled with encouragement). He compared it to the way you'd put a piece of ham between two slices of rye. Thank you, Tom!

If you're looking for a simple way to help your team members grow, I urge you to implement the sandwich technique starting right now. Employees don't like to have their hearts ripped out when they do something wrong. Conversely, they can't progress if they don't know what needs to be corrected. By using this powerful technique, you start and end on a positive note while strategically placing the areas for improvement in the middle.

Many agents have told me the sandwich technique has changed the way they lead. Most importantly, it has caused team members to be more receptive to feedback and growth. It's called leadership through empowerment.

Chris Dorris, an agent in Hoover, Alabama, says: "Never miss a chance to catch a team member doing something right. I'm always thinking about how to get my team members to the next level. I'm a cheerleader but most of all, I'm a team player. My motto is, 'What's best for the team?' If the team wins, everyone wins. Never throw a team member under the bus. I always take the blame because my name is on that sign in the front of the building."

E. G. Warren, an agent in Gulfport, Mississippi, offers this perspective: "So often we think we're empowering people, but we still have them on a leash. I conduct short, stand-up meetings in which I'll brag on someone in front of the entire team. I call them 'little hoorahs.' I might say, 'It has been eight months since anyone did that around here—great work!' Or I'll recognize a particular team member and ask this person to share a certain accomplishment with the team."

Another way to empower people with proper feedback is through the annual employee review. At the Scott Foster Agency, team members are rated on these nine skill sets:

- Efficiency of work
- Quality of work
- Job knowledge
- Attitude
- Appearance
- Adaptability/flexibility
- Initiative
- Communication skills
- Attendance

On each skill set, they receive one of five ratings: 0 = Unsatisfactory, 1 = Below Average, 2 = Satisfactory, 3 = Above Average, 4 = Excellent/Outstanding.

Recognizing And Rewarding Team Members With The Right Incentives

As a team member for an agent, Dan Sevigny was frustrated with the ceiling on his compensation. He went to his boss and asked, "If I can find a way to make you more profitable, would you share it with me?" The agent agreed. Dan developed a pay plan that earned him more than $220,000 in the first year of the new system. He was also an agent for several years before going full-time with his idea.

Dan's powerful compensation program is called PayIgniter™. It's designed to inspire agency team members to break the entitlement attitude and become entrepreneurially minded. The concept removes the notion that a team member's primary job is to punch the clock. It keeps the plan in front of everyone at all times and removes any excuses for poor performance. Team members can see where they are and, most importantly, where they want to go.

"With SalaryValidation™," says Dan, "high producers have the opportunity to make superstar compensation. Mediocre producers receive compensation based on sales, not clock punching. When team members work smarter, they make more money. It also creates an incentive to move clients from service to selling opportunities. Once the team has produced commissions totaling their base monthly salaries, they get to keep any excess earnings. You'll never have to overpay for mediocrity or underpay a superstar."

Dan continues: "As the agent, you're given the ability to track individual team member sales status and receive monthly and annual reporting. With the click of a button, you can see immediately how the agency is doing. You set the percentage rates and validation levels. Imagine your agency working to its maximum capacity while maintaining a rewarding atmosphere for your team."

Note: If you'd like to learn more about this compensation program, contact Dan at PayIgniter, 12415 Bandera Road, Helotes, TX 78023, 210-802-3002, www.payigniter.com.

Tom Davis, an agent in Oxford, Mississippi, is a big proponent of PayIgniter™. "I believe most bonus systems allow team members to make additional money, but the difference with Dan's system is that the team must validate their salary before making a bonus.

I've had team members who, by my standards, weren't selling that much. When we implemented Dan's system, one team member couldn't cut it, but two others more than doubled their production. In fact, both of them have produced more than one hundred apps a month several times."

Tom continues: "This system allows me to pay more per app because you don't get a bonus until you validate your salary. Therefore, each app is worth more. Most agents are trying to make superstars out of average team members and frankly, they haven't had much success. You need salespeople who are motivated by making money. Dan's program can definitely improve average performers, but it's always best to recruit superstars who possess sales ability and self-motivation."

Sully Blair, an agent in Bennettsville, South Carolina, also has created a web-based compensation tool exclusively for the agents of the company he represents. It emulates the annual agency bonus Sully gets if he hits certain levels in all product lines. When team members do the same thing, they get a higher percentage of commission. "If the team gets what it wants, I get what I want. We have no secrets concerning our compensation plan."

P. J. Johnson, an agent in North Charleston, South Carolina, rewards weekly production. "The team members get a weekly bonus if they meet certain production goals. Salespeople tend to be competitive, so it's a team bonus. It provides immediate reinforcement and a sense of accomplishment. If the team hits its bonus every week, we end up with a very productive year."

"I have more than forty different bonus opportunities in my office," says Stan Simmons, an agent in Lawrenceburg, Kentucky. "I want the team members to stretch and fully apply themselves.

They seem to do that when they're compensated well for their extra efforts. It enables us to maximize our potential."

Bill Kolb, an agent in Pryor, Oklahoma, says: "About 95 percent of our P&C commissions were walk-in customers, so the team was picking the low-hanging fruit. We were doing virtually nothing in financial services. So I changed the compensation plan and required team members to sell a minimum number of financial services in order to get their P&C commissions. Production went through the roof because a hungry tiger hunts harder! If your team doesn't have any skin in the game, they'll keep picking the low-hanging fruit until it's all gone and there's nothing left to sustain them."

Fostering Team Loyalty And Minimizing Turnover

Zell Miller, a marine veteran, former US senator, past Georgia governor and author of *Corps Values*, defines loyalty as "the thread which holds together the fabric of humanity." Webster's says loyalty is "unswerving in allegiance" and "the quality or state of being faithful." Whether it's your family, agency or any other organization, loyalty is forged over time and based on mutual trust. Once loyalty is sabotaged and trust is shattered, there's a tendency for people to favor self-sufficiency over teamwork.

Semper fidelis or "always faithful" is the marine motto. It says a lot about the worth of loyalty in the corps. This unique bond is epitomized by the saying, "Once a Marine, always a Marine." There are no ex-marines. It's a tight brotherhood, one that must be experienced to be fully understood. It's also serves as a worthy pattern for fostering loyalty at your agency.

Scott Foster takes loyalty very seriously, and consequently, he's experienced minimal team turnover in his long career. For example, to build a feeling of family, he's taken his team to the Ritz Carlton at nearby Lake Oconee for the weekend. He's taken his team to a nice restaurant via limousine so they wouldn't have to drive in Atlanta traffic. "Of course, doing these types of things can work both ways. You can't do enough for some people (they love it.) You can't do enough for some people (they'll complain no matter what)."

Scott also has a very generous compensation package for his team members. It includes paid personal time (up to twenty-five days for ten years of service), holiday pay (eight days), maternity leave, death and bereavement leave, liberal bonuses, a 401(k) plan (after one year of service), and reimbursement for expenses associated with team member development.

Perry Olson is an agent with locations in Las Vegas and Henderson, Nevada. Only thirty-five, Perry has been an agent for just seven years and has eighteen team members. "I've only had to fire one person. And I've only had one person leave me. She wanted to be with her boyfriend in another town. All of my people are young. Some have never had another a job or worked for minimum wage. I take care of my team members because they make our agencies possible."

Perry continues: "I provide health insurance to every team member. I have a 401(k) and match it with a 3 percent contribution. I pay for day care. Actually, the team pays for day care by chipping in a nominal amount each month. We don't want any excuses for someone not showing up at work. I've cosigned six car loans for team members and never been burned. I offer an annual bonus, which amounts to about $6,500 per person. I encourage them to go to school because it's all about betterment."

"I have thirteen team members," says Steve Cannon, an agent in Woodstock, Georgia, "and four of them have been with me fifteen to twenty-three years. I care about them and their families. I offer a lot of benefits and perks. For example, team members get extra days off for birthdays, Christmas and other special occasions. I have their cars washed every month. I buy them lunch and surprise them with gift cards. The team is my asset, an extension of me."

Isabelle Waldrep, an agent in Forsyth, Georgia, has an interesting way to foster loyalty. "My team members work four days a week, 8 a.m.–6 p.m. Our senior team member is off on Monday. Another team member is off on Tuesday. Two others are off on Thursday. I take off on Friday when the entire team is here. The only time we have everyone on board is Wednesday, which is when we have our team meetings."

Isabelle continues: "I don't have a problem with team members showing up for work because they only have four days to get the job done. They've even trained their customers to know what days they'll be off. This system keeps the team engaged and is a big morale booster. Some of my team members make as much in commissions/bonuses as their base salary. We've had this four-day system in place for four and a half years, so I'd probably have a team rebellion if we returned to a five-day workweek."

"The team must feel like it's a part of the agency," states Ray Cornprobst, a retired field leader in The Villages, Florida. "If the agent does well, the team members should also do well. Tie your compensation to the team's compensation. Learn to say 'we' and 'ours' instead of 'me' and 'mine' when talking about the agency. You want the agency culture to be less individualistic and more like a cohesive team."

To determine what drives work-force loyalty, AON Consulting surveyed more than 1,800 employers and discovered seventeen key drivers of optimal employee retention. The top five are as follows:

Recognize the importance of personal and family time. No matter how dedicated your team may be, they need adequate time to rejuvenate, reflect, relax and relish their relationships outside of the agency.

Emphasize the direction of the organization. It's the leader's job to cast the vision so that the team buys in completely to the big picture of where the agency is headed.

Provide opportunities for personal growth. If you want your agency to reach its full potential, you and your team need a specific plan for personal growth and professional development.

Ensure that people derive satisfaction from everyday work. Boredom has no place in your agency. Keep things fresh by offering a pleasing workplace environment, a competitive atmosphere, stimulating incentive plans and a positive attitude.

Encourage people to challenge the ways things are done. Only insecure leaders discourage team members from speaking their minds on how to make things better. The fear of retaliation for speaking up is a poor strategy for continuous improvement.

Remember: If you want greater work-force loyalty at your agency, you must value people more than profits. Faithful, trustworthy team members tend to produce abundant profits. Abundant profits enable your agency to succeed over the long haul.

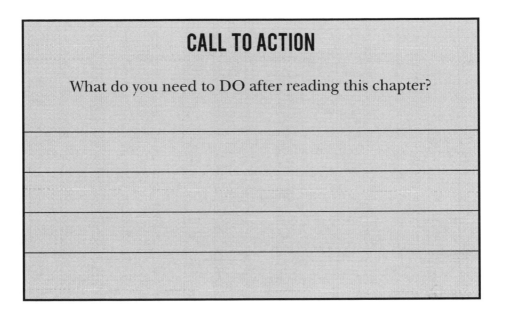

CALL TO ACTION

What do you need to DO after reading this chapter?

Chapter 15

ATTAINING A DREAM TEAM

"Low performers…drive away your superstars. They bring middle performers down to their level and force everyone to pick up the slack in order to serve customers properly."
–Quint Studer, *Results That Last*

Theme:
Are you guiding your associates to new heights of success and happiness?

Key Points:
- Treating team members with respect and dignity
- Accepting that team members have personal lives
- Encouraging team members to challenge the process

If you're a serious basketball fan and old enough to remember the Dream Team from the 1992 Summer Olympics in Barcelona, Spain, did you ever doubt that these twelve super stars would win the gold medal for America? Not likely.

The Naismith Memorial Basketball Hall Of Fame called Michael Jordan, Magic Johnson, Larry Bird, Charles Barkley, David Robinson, John Stockton, Karl Malone, Scottie Pippen, Chris Mullin, Clyde Drexler, Patrick Ewing and Christian Laettner the "greatest collection of basketball talent on the planet." They dominated eight opponents, winning by nearly forty-four points per game.

Admittedly, this was a special team for a special occasion, but why wouldn't you want a dream team working with you every day? Why be content with average? Glenn Parker said it well in *Teamwork*: "You can't have a high-performing team with low-talent team members." Alas, many agents settle for mediocre associates who produce mediocre results year after year.

A few years ago, Scott Foster invited me to speak to his team at their annual agency planning retreat. In preparing for this meeting, I talked extensively with Scott's team captains to help determine my program content. Based on their input, I developed a presentation entitled "The Five Greatest Traits Of An Agency Team Member," which has since been delivered to several agency teams. Perhaps this will be helpful in assembling your dream team:

A great team member keeps a positive perspective. Negative team members tend to bring everyone else down to their level. A positive outlook is essential in embracing the inevitability of change and creating the right agency atmosphere.

A great team member masters the art of self-discipline. Team members should be prompt. They should be self-starters. They should go the extra mile by coming in early or staying late when necessary. They should be reliable. They should work hard and be peak performers.

A great team member maintains laser-sharp focus. Team members must be able to chip away persistently at their daily priorities. They must be able to tune out distractions and concentrate on the achievement of the agency's annual goals.

A great team member embraces ongoing growth. The team should be committed to lifelong learning. Don't tolerate someone with a know-it-all attitude. Team members are either developing or deteriorating.

A great team member welcomes accountability. High-character people expect to be held responsible for their actions. If you hire team members with sound values, you won't have to worry about your agency's reputation.

Frankly, you're probably better off with a team member who barely made it through high school and possesses all five of these qualities than with a college graduate who's missing two or three of these traits. Of course, if you can hire college graduates who are positive, disciplined, focused, eager to learn and open to accountability, you have a potential dream team.

Treating Team Members With Respect And Dignity

I often ask business leaders this question: What's more important in your company—people or profits? I've never had a leader say "profits." However, if you look at companies that are downsizing, the first thing to go is usually people. Now, I realize a company has to be profitable to stay in business, but what makes profit possible in the first place? The obvious answer is a dedicated group of people who are treated with respect and dignity.

Cliff Ourso, an agent in Donaldsonville, Louisiana, declares: "The 'Golden Rule' shouldn't just apply to our personal lives; it should apply to businesses as well. If you treat people badly, you'll be treated badly. I strive to treat my team like family. We don't have to like each other—although we should—but we do have to work together."

Cliff continues: "In the real world, there's going to be some conflict. We don't let disagreements fester. We put everyone in a room, talk it out and get resolution. Sometimes we just have to agree to disagree. If there's a personality issue, I bring in both parties and say, 'I can fix this, but one of you isn't going to like the results. Either let it go or I'll let you go.'"

The Scott Foster Agency has something called the 'Sunshine System.' It's designed to help team members when they're getting married, suffering an illness, grieving the loss of a loved one or some other personal situation. "We deliver flowers or a meal to their home. It's our way of showing we care about our people. We try to work as hard at keeping our team members as we do at recruiting them."

Birthdays are also celebrated once a month at Scott's agency. "We bring in food and have a good time. We do a lot of little things to show appreciation. We also build team camaraderie with our 'Thanksgiving Project.' We deliver pies or jellies to customers who've suffered some trauma in their lives—a bad car accident, home fire or something like that."

Accepting That Team Members Have Personal Lives

Tony Pope is an agent with locations in Summerville and Mount Pleasant, South Carolina. He has twenty team members, and many of them have been with him for fifteen to twenty years. "I'm fairly flexible on allowing team members to be with their kids. One team member goes to lunch at 2:00 p.m. so she can pick up her children at school. I once got a note from a kid thanking me for allowing his mother to be there when school was over."

Brooks Baltich, an agent in Richmond, Virginia, hired a team member who was a processes specialist. "She had what's known as a Six Sigma Green Belt, one of a series of earned degrees for process improvement. She was working full-time but wanted to continue her education. She asked if she could work part-time and go back to school. I didn't want to throw the baby out with the bathwater, so I agreed. In the long run, it was best for everyone."

Kirk Baker, an agent in Valencia, California, had an aspirant—a team member who wants to become an agent—whose father was dying of brain cancer. "I try to expose my aspirants to everything we do in the office. I'm also big on aspirants obtaining their security licenses. This young man failed the exam four times. He wasn't in the right frame of mind to study, but he had only one shot left to get it right. I told him to take whatever time he needed to be with his father and prepare properly for the exam. He realized I cared about him, and it turned into a good bonding experience."

Cliff Ourso, an agent in Donaldsonville, Louisiana, says: "I tell my team members, 'You're working here because I need you.' Obviously, there are going to be times when team members have to be away from the agency for personal matters. I give everyone twelve personal days a year, plus vacation. I want them to take time off, but we can't have someone abusing the rules. I'll dock someone's paycheck if a situation gets out of hand. It's rare when all ten team members are on board. But if we don't have at least seven people at the agency, it's a nightmare."

Dan Combs, an agent in Dalton, Georgia, includes work/life balance in the agency's values statement. "It's God, family and work, in that order. We're definitely a faith-based organization. We pray regularly as an agency. I don't expect my team members to work as hard as I do, but I expect them to be professional at all times."

"When your personal life is messed up," says Steve Cannon, an agent in Woodstock, Georgia, "so is your professional life. We can't neglect the important things of life and expect them to get better. I try to influence my team members, including their time away from the agency. It's an investment that's well worth it."

Encouraging Team Members To Challenge The Process

Andy Stanley, senior pastor at North Point Ministries in Alpharetta, Georgia, once delivered a message entitled "Challenging The Process." **The gist of his presentation:** Caring leaders want their people to tell them how to make things better. It's the way good organizations become great organizations. It's how good leaders become great leaders.

What about your agency? Are you willing to let your team challenge the process? Sam Eubank, a field leader in Newburgh, New York, maintains: "Every agency process needs to be challenged—not in an adversarial way, but by asking, 'Does it fit?' It's healthy to have different streams of thought within an agency. Agents need to empower their teams with the freedom to say when something doesn't fit and what changes need to be made."

If you won't allow the agency process to be challenged by your team, why won't you? Is it insecurity? Is it embarrassment? Is it a dislike for transparency? Is it a desire to avoid confrontation? Is it the fear of losing control? Is it because you're crippled by fear? Is it a comfort zone mentality? Your agency can't reach its full potential if you're unwilling to try some new ways of doing things or unable to discard some old things that are inefficient.

The Scott Foster Agency employee manual says: "Scott welcomes any and all ideas and suggestions you may have. Please do not hesitate to let them be known. We welcome all employee contributions. Changes will be made when an idea merits a change and is beneficial to a majority of the team and management, or to our clients."

Scott isn't so thin-skinned that he can't accept constructive feedback. He realizes there's always room for improvement. During his annual review with each employee, he asks questions like these:

- What changes do we need to make next year?
- What are our strengths?
- Where do you envision yourself (professionally) this time next year?
- What are the obstacles that will prevent you from meeting your goals next year?
- Is there anything I need to do to help you reach your goals?
- How can I help you perform better?
- How am I progressing as your leader?
- Is there anything you've been meaning to tell or ask me?
- If you could change something about your career, what would it be?
- If you could build a perfect day here, what would it look like?

Great leaders know they don't have all the answers and welcome the views of their associates. It results in the team respecting you more for your transparency and adaptability. Moreover, the team appreciates the opportunity to voice their views without retribution. Most of all, your agency will grow and get better because you were brave enough to allow the process to be challenged.

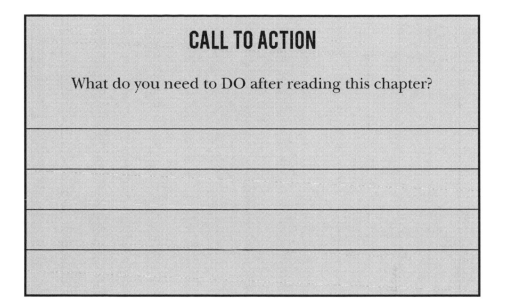

TIER 4:
THE TEACHING-BASED LEADER

It's about people development and peak performance

Modeling The Way

Motivating Vs. Inspiring

Mentoring Your Protégés

Maintaining Accountability

Multiplying Your Influence

Chapter 16:
MODELING THE WAY

"Every man's work…is always a portrait of himself, and the more
he tries to conceal himself, the more clearly his character will
appear in spite of him."
–Samuel J. Butler, *The Way Of All Flesh*

Theme:
Do you consistently replicate the behavior you want your team to emulate?

Key Points:
- Role modeling isn't optional
- There's no substitute for congruent behavior
- The high price of leadership

Stephen Gower, a speaker from Toccoa, Georgia, once asked this provocative question at a Georgia Speakers Association meeting: What do they see when they see you coming? Stephen was challenging his peers to "walk their talks," but is it any different for you as an agency leader?

At a seminar in Florida years ago, an agent said during an interactive part of the training, "Dick, I love your ideas, but if I implemented just half of them, I couldn't play golf three times a week." I didn't say anything—after all, it's his business—but here's what I was thinking: "Your team probably believes that playing golf is more important to you than leading your agency."

As an independent business owner, you can choose to be an absentee owner, a fully engaged agent or somewhere in between. However, if you're not around most of the time, are you modeling leadership at the highest level? Your physical presence speaks volumes about your leadership commitment. In your absence, most likely a team member will fill the leadership void, a situation that could take your agency in an unintended direction.

I'm not saying you don't deserve some time away from the agency. You definitely do! Take your vacations, long weekend getaways and award trips. Go to off-site training sessions. Volunteer in your community. Participate in social and sports activities. Accept some opportunities to speak to your peers. These are important outside activities, but shouldn't they be balanced with your leadership responsibilities?

Scott Foster put modeling in its proper perspective one day at lunch: "Dick, I could be gone from the agency for six months and we wouldn't miss a beat. However, I love this business and feel an obligation to be with the team as much as possible." Scott knows his team members are more likely to love what they do when their leader is setting a congruent example. In other words, Scott is striving to replicate the behavior he wants his team to emulate.

Role Modeling Isn't Optional

Bill Kolb, an agent in Pryor, Oklahoma, states: "A big part of being a role model is the attitude you project to your team. This is why it's important to avoid negative thinkers. They're a distraction. They like to drag you down to their level. They always blame someone else for their problems. It infects you and your team by creating doubt. As the leader, I want to project the most positive example possible."

P. J. Johnson, an agent in North Charleston, South Carolina, contends: "When you think you're too good to do the jobs of your team members, they can tell. I can quote any product in this office. The team needs to know that I understand the processes they're dealing with every day. I meet with customers to discover their preferences and establish a personal connection. You can't do this if you're an **MIA**—missing insurance agent! This shouldn't be a hobby."

I've met a lot of agents who are absentee owners, but observed very few top producers who aren't actively and consistently on-site. If you really love your profession, why wouldn't you want to meet regularly with the team? With the exception of a personal health crisis, a dying loved one or some other critical concern, why would you be away for prolonged periods of time? Moreover, why would you expect your team to work hard every day when you're more devoted to playing golf, running another business or traveling constantly?

Perhaps you're thinking you deserve to be an absentee owner because you've done such a good job of getting the right team in place. If that's true, why wouldn't you want to be there to witness your handiwork in action? Could it be that you enjoy the freedom of entrepreneurship, but you're circumventing the full-time responsibility of leadership?

Christine Bailey, an agent in Moss Bluff, Louisiana, asserts: "You have to lead by example. There's something about me sitting at my desk that gives the team security, confidence and more push to get things done. My presence says, 'This business matters to me!' How can I expect my team to work forty or more hours a week when I'm unwilling to do the same? It shouts, 'I don't care!' The team members might not say it, but they're thinking: Why is the boss somewhere else and we're here?"

Cliff Ourso, an agent in Donaldsonville, Louisiana, shared this keen observation: "Absentee leadership rarely works unless an agent can delegate tasks and responsibilities with a high degree of accountability. A team tends to take on the approach of the agent. An agent needs to be engaged in developing the desired philosophy and training the team. It's very difficult for agents to do less and less and accomplish more and more until eventually they do nothing and accomplish everything."

Doug Nichols, an agent in Knoxville, Tennessee, says: "I'm running the agency; it's not running me. I'm proud to be a hands-on agent. If you're an involved leader, you'll meet regularly with your team. You can't do that if you're gone all the time. A lot of agents are in the business, but the business isn't in them."

There's No Substitute For Congruent Behavior

The late Cavett Robert, founder of the National Speakers Association, loved to tell this story about his native state:

Back in the days of Prohibition, the editor of a small Mississippi newspaper had the unmitigated gall to ask a politician up for reelection how he felt about the whiskey issue. The politician, knowing he'd probably get half the votes if he was for whiskey, and half the votes if he was against whiskey, acquitted himself in a most admirable fashion when he wrote back to the editor and said:

Sir, I had not planned to discuss this controversial question at this time, but far be it from me to sidestep any issue regardless of the nature and result. So I want to be sure I understand you now. If, sir, when you say whiskey, you mean that devil's brew, that poison scourge, that bloody monster that defiles innocence, dethrones reason, creates misery and poverty, yeah, it takes the very bread out of the mouths of babes.

If, sir, when you say whiskey, if you mean that vile drink that topples Christian men and women from the pinnacles of righteous and gracious living and into the bottomless pit of despair, deprivation, shame, hopelessness, helplessness, destroys homes, creates orphans and depraves the community in general. Then, sir, if that's what you mean by whiskey, I want you to put this in your newspaper: I promise my constituents that if I'm reelected, I'll fight to destroy this demon with all the strength that I possess.

BUT, on the other hand, when you say whiskey, if you mean that oil of conversation, that philosophic wine and ale that's consumed when good folks get together, that puts a song in their hearts, laughter on their lips, and warm contentment in their eyes. Well, sir, when you say whiskey, if you mean that nectar of the gods, the sale of which puts untold millions in our treasury, and tenderly cares for our little orphan children, builds our schools, hospitals and highways, and makes this world a better place to live.

Well, sir, if that's what you mean by whiskey, I want you to put this in your newspaper: I promise my constituents that if I'm reelected, I'll fight to protect this essence of divinity with all the strength that I possess.

And then I thought the politician added the crowning climax, the capstone of it all, when he said: Sir, now that I've answered your question without equivocation, I hope you'll in good conscience agree that I'm a man with the courage of convictions. I will not compromise. This is my stand!

Obviously, you can't have it both ways and be a congruent leader. To be congruent is to "be in agreement or harmony." If you don't set a worthy, consistent example as a leader, how can you expect your team to take you seriously? If your words are saying one thing but your actions are saying something else, you're displaying incongruent leadership.

The High Price Of Leadership

Great leaders have paid their dues for the privilege of influencing others. The price is responsibility. Responsible leaders know they're always being observed. They realize their behavior influences the people around them. Never allow arrogance and contentment to sabotage your influence.

Jon Gordon, author of *Training Camp, The Energy Bus* and other best-selling books, offers some wise advice to leaders in an article entitled "Humble & Hungry." He graciously gave us permission to reprint his message on why arrogance and contentment should be avoided:

"I've found that two words are the key to a life and career of continuous improvement and growth. Whether you're just starting out, you're making a name for yourself, or you're at the pinnacle of success, it's important to remember to be humble and hungry."

Be humble

- Don't think you know it all. See yourself as a lifelong learner who is always seeking ways to learn, grow and improve.
- See everyone as a teacher and learn from everyone you meet.
- Be open to new ideas and strategies to take your life, school and work to the next level.
- When people tell you that you're great, don't let it go to your head. When they tell you that you stink, don't let it go to your head.
- Be kind to everyone and let people know they matter.
- Live with humility because the minute you think you've arrived at the door of greatness, it will get shut in your face.
- Humility doesn't mean you think less of yourself. It just means you think of yourself less.

Be hungry

- Follow your passion, continuously improve and continue to dream.
- Seek out new ideas, new strategies and new ways to push yourself out of your comfort zone.
- Invest the time, energy, sweat and dedication to be your best, and let God do the rest.
- Be willing to pay the price that greatness requires. Don't be average. Strive to be great.
- Become the hardest worker you know.
- Love the process, and you'll love what the process produces.
- Decide to leave a legacy. Even at a young age, it's important to think about what legacy you want to leave because knowing how you want to be remembered helps you decide how to live today.
- Don't focus on where you've been. Focus on where you are and where you're going.
- Make your life and work a quest for excellence. Ask every day, "How I can be better today than I was yesterday?"
- Make your next work your best work.

Jon concludes: "As I share this advice, my hope is that these words will move you to action. Regardless of your age, education or career status, if you stay *Humble & Hungry*, everything else will take care of itself."

The Georgia field leader who sent me Jon's article also shared these thoughts on the high price of leadership:

Sense of purpose—Great agents don't wake up to an alarm clock; they wake up to a calling. They know why they do what they do.

Moreover, they understand how all of the pieces of the agency puzzle fit together.

Situational awareness—Great agents see complexities as opportunities to shine. For example, if a disaster strikes, they'll be there for their customers. In turn, customers will be talking about their agents for years to come.

Political involvement—Great agents don't wait for a law to be passed that adversely impacts their profession. They're proactive now. They're involved in matters that can change everything about the way they do business in their state.

Resource leverage—Great agents take full advantage of every support team at their disposal, internally and externally. They don't have to be a subject matter expert, but they should be a relationship expert.

Ego management—Great agents aren't boastful. When they say, "I make too much money," it creates a false sense of pride and lures them into thinking they're smarter than they really are. This attitude often keeps them from reaching their full potential.

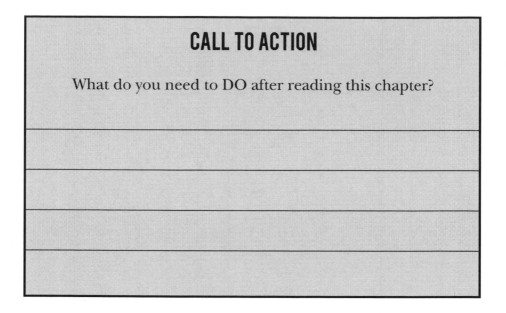

CALL TO ACTION

What do you need to DO after reading this chapter?

Chapter 17:
MOTIVATING VS. INSPIRING

"You cannot push anyone up a ladder unless
he is willing to climb it himself."
–Andrew Carnegie

Theme:
Are you intimidating or stimulating your team to get the desired results?

Key Points:
- Motivating with a stick
- Inspiring with a carrot
- Excelling through self-motivation

We arrived at Parris Island, South Carolina, for Marine Corps boot camp late in the evening of October 20, 1964. Still in our civilian clothes early the next morning, our group of frightened recruits was escorted to the mess hall. As we waited outside in the darkness for our turn to eat breakfast, I heard an unforgettable rhythmic sound in the distance: thud...thud...thud...thud. Overwhelmed by curiosity, I turned to see what was making this unusual but awesome reverberation.

It was a veteran platoon marching in perfect formation to the baritone cadence of its drill instructor (DI). The thud...thud...thud... thud was the boot heels of seventy-five recruits striking the asphalt pavement with astonishing synchronization. Alas, my admiration quickly turned to terror as the DI of this veteran platoon rushed toward me, put his mouth up to my ear and yelled some nasty things that won't be repeated here.

Suffice it to say, that DI wasn't trying to stimulate me. It was pure intimidation and yes, I got the message loud and clear. Our bad habits were going to be changed through motivation by force and fear. After all, we were a ragtag group of immature teenagers who needed a big dose of discipline if we were to become US Marines.

Now, I know you aren't leading a military organization, but have you analyzed your leadership style lately? Hopefully, you're not "motivating" your team through force and fear. Most mature adults respond better to inspiration. If you have people who aren't self-motivated, why are they on your team? My friend Buddy Brown used to say it crudely but quite accurately: "You can't make chicken salad out of chicken manure!"

As mentioned previously, words have meaning. It's like saying "North Dakota" when you mean "North Carolina." Yes, both are American states, but there are big differences in geography, climate, population, culture and more. Likewise, the words "inspiration" and "motivation" are often used interchangeably, but they have entirely different meanings.

Inspiration is "any stimulus to creative thought." It's having the right *mental* outlook, which is influenced greatly by *external* forces. This is why it's so important to make wise choices concerning your circle of influence. Who are your friends? Who are your mentors? What type of organizations do you belong to? What are you reading? What are you listening to? What are you watching? Your choice of influencers is critical.

Conversely, motivation is "some inner drive, impulse or intention that causes a person to do something or act in a certain way." It's having the *internal* drive and *physical* energy to make something happen. There's good reason for the term *self-motivation* because it must come from within.

I've delivered hundreds of presentations in all fifty states and several foreign countries and never referred to myself as a motivational speaker. Yet when people learn about my profession, they usually ask, "Oh, are you a motivational speaker?" Bluntly, "motivational" sounds arrogant and misguided. I'm not a miracle worker. My responsibility is to inspire and inform people at the highest level. It's up to the program participants to be self-motivated to take action because I can't make a group of grown-ups DO anything.

Ironically, meeting planners still invite me to "motivate" their people. Sometimes I have fun by asking two questions: "First, after I do my program, how long do you want your people to be motivated?" Most of the time, the meeting planners answer, "Every day."

"Second, since you want your people to be 'motivated' all the time, are you prepared to hire me every working day for the next year?" Meeting planners usually laugh and respond, "That would take too much time and cost too much money. What do you charge to inspire our employees for a day?"

Motivating With A Stick

As a rule, children and young adults need a good dose of motivation by force and fear because they're often immature and irresponsible. My parents spanked me (force) and threatened to ground me (fear) when I behaved badly. My boot camp DIs used the same tactics, but at a more intense level. In those days, marine DIs carried swagger sticks, which were covered in leather and tipped with metal at each end. While mostly for show, these symbols of authority certainly got our attention.

It reminds me of Thurman Askew. He married Thelma Biggs, my mother, many years after my parents divorced. Thurman worked as a supervisor for a small chain of grocery stores in Georgia. When visiting these locations, Thurman would tell the employees what he expected them to do. He'd often say, "If the job isn't done right, I'll be back with my damn two-by-four." Thurman used his imaginary visual aid to let everyone know he meant business.

At his retirement party, one of Thurman's gifts was a real wooden stick with this caption: "Damn 2x4!" It's now displayed proudly in his room at the Nancy Hart Nursing Center where he and my mother reside in their nineties. While Thurman credits a lot of his career success to motivating with a stick, you should know that he was dealing with many undisciplined employees in some tough places.

Imagine how your team would feel if you displayed a big stick at your agency. You'd probably have a difficult time hiring new team members. It's also likely that a "Damn 2x4" approach would intimidate your current employees. So even if you don't have a menacing piece of lumber hanging on your office wall, I trust that you aren't motivating with a stick to get the desired results.

Inspiring With A Carrot

Hopefully, you have an extremely inspired agency team. If so, it's probably because your associates respond better to stimulation than intimidation. To intimidate is "to make timid or fearful... to threaten...to bully, browbeat or bulldoze." To stimulate is "to

excite to activity or growth." That's quite a contrast in le
styles, wouldn't you agree?

Art Brucks, an agent in Burleson, Texas, laughs when talking about
team inspiration. "I like to have three levels of goals for my team
members. First, there are the 'I'll be fired' goals for not reaching
certain minimum production levels. Second, there are the goals I
expect you to achieve. Third, there are the 'shoot for the moon'
goals. I pay higher bonuses for higher production. We track activity, so I can see what each team member is doing at any time."

Bill Kolb, an agent in Pryor, Oklahoma, likes to inspire his team
members with "an old-school production board in the conference
room. We have computer production reports coming out of our
ears, but they can be deleted. The team can't escape that whiteboard because we're in the conference room a lot. Each team
member writes down his or her production numbers during the
day. We go over it in our weekly team meetings. It's a great accountability tool. When we see a big sale on the board, we go straight to
this team member and offer congratulations."

Another way to inspire your team members is with exciting weekly
meetings. These sessions should be a two-way forum of exchange.
First, team members should give progress reports on their specific
agency goals. It's astounding how many agents don't make this a
required discipline and wonder why holding the team accountable is such a weakness. Second, you should provide encouragement and hope by creating an environment of high energy and
expectations.

Here's what Terri Phillips, contact center training manager for
a major insurance company, recommends for agency meetings:
"Find out what inspires the team by knowing their strengths and

passions. Team members tend to stay involved when they're engaged. Bring in outside speakers from time to time. Consider having daily huddles with your team—and keep the main thing the main thing. Cast the vision continuously because it can't be communicated enough. Finally, if your meetings were videotaped, would you be proud of them?"

To produce more inspiring team meetings, follow these guidelines:

Start on time. Otherwise, you penalize the people who are prompt.

Be prepared. Have an agenda and stick to it.

Invite team participation. Don't allow one person to dominate the meeting.

Spice things up. Use humor. Tell a riveting story. Do a skit. Listen to a stirring audio message. Watch a compelling video clip.

Avoid boring activities. Don't read long passages that can be perused later. Don't digress and waste valuable time. Don't put up slide after slide and say, "I know you can't see this but...." If it can't be read, why is it up there?

Be results oriented. It makes everyone feel good about attending.

End on time. It says that you respect the schedules of everyone.

Follow up. Accountability stimulates action.

Gary Welch, an agent in Peoria, Illinois, says: "At this point in my career, what I need the most is inspiration. Show me an agent that isn't a successful business owner and, most of the time, you'll find it's someone lacking inspiration. I believe inspirational leadership is the one thing that can move agents to more productive levels."

Key questions: How are you being inspired? How are you inspiring your team?

Sully Blair, an agent in Bennettsville, South Carolina, takes this approach to inspiration: "I meet every morning with my team. I call them cheerleading sessions. We review our goals. I don't beat them up with promotions. I just stress consistency in all product lines every month—and that's exactly what we get. I'm very passionate about my team, very open about everything. It produces greater commitment. I think my team members feel like their names are on that sign outside the office, not just mine."

Another agent who knows how to inspire a team is David Wilcox in Gonzales, Louisiana: "We have something called a 'Millionaire Trip.' Team members who sell at least $1 million of face-amount life insurance in a year earn a free trip. We've been skiing in Colorado. We've been to the mountains in Tennessee and Arkansas. We've been on cruises. We've gone trout fishing. It's a big goal but for some team members, it's better than a pay raise."

Excelling Through Self-Motivation

If you aren't a self-motivated leader, how can you expect your team members to be ambitious? Here are ten tips for being a more driven agent, thanks to Don Rood Jr., a field leader in Los Angeles, California:

Make time to think about the agency. This was covered in chapter 1, but it's probably the most important thing you can do to grow your book of business. To reiterate, find a *quiet place* to reflect on what the agency is doing right, and look for specific ways to get better. Establish a *consistent time* for contemplation—weekly, monthly, quarterly or whatever time works best for you—and be sure to turn your thoughts into action.

Be intentional or you'll unintentionally do things you shouldn't do. An agent once said to me, "Dick, are you always so intentional?" Listen: you only live once, so why waste any time being unintentional? If you've developed some bad habits, replace them with more intentional patterns of behavior. By the way, my next project is a gift book entitled *Be Intentional Today: Ten Truths For More Purposeful Living.*

Commit to constant leadership development. Are you spending too much time selling and servicing, and less time leading and mentoring? You can hire sales and service people, but only you can guide the agency. Are you a dedicated student of leadership? Are you an exemplary role model? Are you making time to mentor your team members?

Cast a bold, broad and bright vision for the agency. This is even more critical than your annual business plan. It's your responsibility to cast the vision for where the agency wants to be in the next five years and beyond. This doesn't happen accidentally. Your team members expect you to chart the course of the agency. Don't they deserve to know the direction they're headed?

Narrow your focus with a dynamic annual business plan and let it become a living, breathing document every working day. This was covered in chapter 7, but the idea is to create the plan annually, work the plan daily, track your goals weekly and celebrate your successes quarterly.

Change the structure of the agency to gain, train, sustain and retain good people. In countless discussions I've had with agents over the years, team issues are always the toughest challenge. It's hard to gain good people but once they're on board, you must purposefully and persistently train, sustain and retain your team members. Otherwise, expect a substantially high turnover, increased costs and unnecessary tension.

Define the role of each team member, offer frequent encouragement and reward generously for peak performance. Prepare written instructions for each team member's responsibilities. Be an encourager. Most importantly, set up a generous pay plan to reward peak performance. Don't tolerate subpar performance by continuing to pay dearly for underachievement.

Create ownership by allowing team members to be a part of the decision-making process. Yes, you have the final say in all agency decisions, but it's also true that you can't operate the business alone. Ask team members what they think. When feasible, implement their ideas and give them credit. Trainer Bob Pike says, "People don't argue with their own information."

Build strong relationships with agency partners. Tap into the wealth of knowledge and experience from any available resources, internal and external. Why fly solo when there are many seasoned copilots available to help you soar successfully? There's truly power in collaboration and collective thinking. Even the "Lone" Ranger had Tonto.

Use cutting-edge technology to help the agency become more efficient and effective. This is a no-brainer. Alas, to their detriment, many agents have resisted the pace and volume of change in technology. Could it be that the mental battle is more about deciding to change rather than implementing the changes?

As a self-motivated leader, you should hire team members with the same internal drive. Here are some of the best agency practices for inspiring team members to a greater level of self-motivation:

- Make time for team members.
- Give team members a sense of ownership.
- Involve team members in the decision-making process.
- Reward team members for peak performance.
- Give team members opportunities for growth.
- Have open communication with team members.
- Use proper feedback to encourage team members.
- Say "thank you" and "good job" as often as possible.
- Share information with team members.
- Celebrate with team members in fun, creative ways.

CALL TO ACTION

What do you need to DO after reading this chapter?

Chapter 18:
MENTORING YOUR PROTÉGÉS

"Our research discovered that an aspirant in a mentoring
relationship is much more likely to survive and prosper. In fact,
most agents we interviewed told us they wouldn't have made it to
MDRT if they hadn't had a mentor."
–Norm Levine, past president of MDRT
and Top of the Table agent

Theme:
Are you using one-on-one leadership to help team members grow?

Key Points:
* Mentoring is optional
* Mentoring is unique
* Mentoring matters

A special mentor-protégé relationship existed during medieval
times. I'm referring to the guilds, which were associations of people with similar interests. There were social, military and religious
guilds, but the most popular ones were groups of merchants and
craftsmen.

There were three classes of members in a merchant guild. A be-
ginner, known as an apprentice, received only room and board in
exchange for his work. The journeyman received pay and often
lived with his master. The master had the exclusive right to buy
raw materials and sell finished products. Anyone could join a guild

by paying the required taxes. Literally, protégés paid their dues for the right to learn from a master in a particular field of interest.

The guilds provided a systematic way for less experienced people to learn firsthand from veterans. This form of on-the-job training thrived into the late 1700s. For example, Ben Franklin learned the printing trade as an apprentice to his older brother. The apprentice often worked seven years or longer before becoming a journeyman. A long education was required to become a journeyman, including the making of a masterpiece. Few people reached the level of master, just as few people earn a college degree in today's society.

I'm not suggesting a return to the guilds, but it seems like long-term gratification has become a lost art. We all want to do things our own way, and as quickly as possible. I'm certainly not opposed to creativity and urgency, but there's much we can learn from the masters. They understand why true success isn't earned overnight. They're willing to pay the price. They expect to work for everything they get in life. Most of all, masters are eager to pass on what they know to their protégés.

Mentoring Is Optional

Don't confuse role modeling with mentoring; the two concepts are quite different:

- A role model is "a person whose behavior in a particular role is imitated by others." A mentor is "a trusted counselor, guide, tutor or coach."
- Role modeling ISN'T optional. The question is: Are you setting a positive or negative example? Mentoring IS optional. The question is: If you don't get involved, who will?

- You don't choose to be a role model; you're chosen. You must choose to be a mentor.
- When you're a role model, the primary focus is on you. When you're a mentor, the primary focus is on the protégé.
- The time commitment of a role model is simply the life you lead, with everyone free to observe. The time commitment of a mentor is a deep involvement in the life of the protégé.
- As a role model, you say, "Here's a way to live that you might want to emulate." As a mentor, you say, "Here's a way to live that you might want to emulate...and let me share the details of my journey."

In short, mentoring takes role modeling to the next level by teaching protégés the details of who you *are*, how you *think*, what you've *done* and why you *have* something worth pursuing.

Why wouldn't you say yes to the opportunity to mentor your team members? Pat Healey, an agent in Oswego Lake, Oregon, and author of *The Employee Attraction And Retention System*, is a big believer in the mentoring or coaching concept: "Coaching isn't about motivation; it's about managing desire."

Healey elaborates with his "chance, change, cheer" approach to coaching: "Look for *chances* to coach. Identify what is possible to *change*. When an employee seems ready to apply your coaching, it's time for a *cheer*. Unfortunately, it has been my experience... that almost all small business owners have little or no training in this area of business expertise."

How do you know if your mentoring/coaching is effective? Healey has developed this useful checklist, which he gave us permission to share with you:

____ My boss knows when I need help and is able to give me the direction I need.

____ My boss gives me positive feedback on a regular basis.

____ My boss takes the time each week to coach me on things as they occur in real time.

____ My boss never makes me feel stupid or wrong; instead my boss emphasizes the positive changes I can make.

____ My boss is good at explaining what is expected of me and helping me to find ways to achieve these objectives.

____ My boss encourages me to take more initiative and offer my own solutions to problems.

____ In our one-on-one, formal coaching sessions, my boss treats me with respect.

____ In these sessions, I understand what our common goal is and leave knowing what steps to take next.

____ In these sessions, I feel understood and listened to.

____ My skills have grown thanks to the coaching sessions with my boss.

____ Thanks to coaching from my boss, I am experiencing less stress and more joy at work.

____ My boss has helped me to have better relationships with my team members.

___ Because of the coaching I've received from my boss, I have a better understanding of how I am wired and why I do some of the things I do.

___ Coaching has helped me be more efficient and productive without feeling extra pressure.

___ Coaching has helped me better understand our customers and how to meet their needs.

Total number of items checked _____

Do you have the audacity to use this checklist with your team? Moreover, do you have the will to take action based on the feedback you receive?

Mentoring Is Unique

The word "mentor" comes from Greek mythology and Homer's *Iliad*. When you were in school, you may have read about Odysseus, the king of Ithaca. When Odysseus left to fight the Trojan War, he placed Telemachus, his son, in the care of a close friend, Mentor. Odysseus had no way of knowing he'd be gone for ten years, but he was wise enough to ask a trusted friend to care for his boy. Obviously, it had to be a special relationship between Odysseus and Mentor, and between Mentor and Telemachus.

Unlike large-scale leadership, in which the CEO is responsible for several hundred or thousand employees, mentoring is one-on-one leadership—the pairing up of a less experienced person (protégé) with a more seasoned person (mentor) for the purpose of forging a special bond to foster mutual growth.

Indeed, mentoring is unique because it's highly personal. When a mentor spends time with a protégé, they get to know each other at a deeper level provided the relationship is based on trust and openness. If you have such a relationship with your team members, please accept my congratulations. If not, it's never too late to change and get more involved in helping your team members reach their full potential through mentoring.

Scott Garvey, an agent in Baltimore, Maryland, has an astute approach to mentoring his eight aspirants—or team members who want to become agents. Scott publishes a monthly email newsletter entitled *Developmental Agent/Entrepreneur Program*. Scott praises the achievements of his aspirants and sends this publication to a select mailing list. He features the names and photos of each aspirant, words of encouragement and a production breakdown—number of quotes, total premium quoted, sold quotes, total apps by product line and total premium sold.

Bill Thorp, an agent in Grants Pass, Oregon, is an advocate of mentoring. "It's something I've done all my life through teaching, training and sharing. It's one of the best ways you can touch someone's life in a meaningful manner. I remember a young agent coming to me who wanted to make MDRT. I let him know it was a goal he could accomplish. When this agent qualified for MDRT, I was the first person he called. It doesn't get much better than that."

Steve Cannon, an agent in Woodstock, Georgia, states: "I'm big on mentoring. Too many agents bring in people, drive them to sell and then fire them when they don't produce. You have to spend time with your team members if you want them to develop and meet your expectations. I want mentoring to be a part of my legacy. Hopefully, people will look back and say, 'I worked for Steve and he made a difference in my life.'"

Mentoring Matters

How valuable are mentors? I'm a professional speaker and author thanks mainly to Miss Eloise Penn, my English teacher, newspaper adviser and speech coach for three years at East Atlanta High School. Evidently, Miss Penn overlooked my history of poor grades and focused on my potential. Early in my sophomore year, Miss Penn said, "Dick, I think you have a talent for writing and speaking. I'd like to help you develop these skills."

I share this story not to toot my own horn but to honor Miss Penn, an extraordinary mentor. I became an A and B student. I was the editor of the *East Echo*, our school newspaper. I won several Optimist Club–sponsored speech contests. I was the class graduation speaker. I received the Atlanta Quarterback Club Award for "outstanding academic and athletic achievement." None of this success would have happened without the dedicated mentoring of Miss Penn.

I'm a connoisseur of master mentors. Anyone with more experience and wisdom than someone else can be a mentor, but master mentors *make* the time to teach their protégés. Along with Miss Penn, my master mentors include Michael Guido, John Maxwell, Jack McDowell, Lamar Matthews, Earl Masters, Andy Hillman, Linda Miles, Staff Sergeant W. A. McLain, my senior drill instructor at Marine Corps boot camp, and coauthor Scott Foster.

It's impossible to put a value on the contributions these men and women have made to my personal growth and professional development. Hopefully, by passing on to my protégés what many caring master mentors have taught me, I'm expressing my eternal gratitude. So I ask you directly: Who are your master mentors? You'd be wise to surround yourself with an experienced group of advisers who can make a big difference in your life and agency.

Here are the four benchmarks to look for in your master mentors:

- **Benchmark I:** Do they pursue what is true?
- **Benchmark II:** Do they turn creeds into deeds?
- **Benchmark III:** Do they use congruence to influence?
- **Benchmark IV:** Do they collect a deep respect?

The first two benchmarks are focused on the *mind-set* of master mentors. They have high standards ("I profess"). They get things done ("I practice"). The last two benchmarks are about *multiplication*. Based on their beliefs and behavior, master mentors can make a meaningful difference in the lives of their protégés ("I proliferate"). Finally, they strive to leave an esteemed legacy as their protégés become mentors and pass on what they've learned ("I prolong").

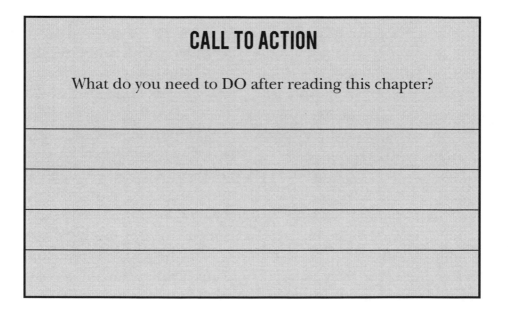

CALL TO ACTION

What do you need to DO after reading this chapter?

Chapter 19:
MAINTAINING ACCOUNTABILITY

"Accountability is a willingness to explain your actions."
–Chuck Swindoll

Theme:
Are you consistently asking team members for progress reports?

Key Points:
- Expectations vs. consequences
- Cooperation vs. confrontation
- Growth vs. stagnation

What's the difference between a good agent and a great one? I once posed this question to numerous agents at all production levels and here's what I discovered: good agents described great agents in terms of *tangible* achievements, such as number of customers and policies, premium dollars, sales awards, big teams, professional designations such as CLU, CPCU and so forth.

On the other hand, great agents viewed themselves more in terms of *intangible* traits, with the following three receiving the most attention: (1) Great agents shun complacency. (2) Great agents minimize procrastination. (3) Great agents welcome accountability. Since the first two leadership qualities have been covered elsewhere, this chapter will address the third trait.

Accountability is problematic for many agents for two reasons: First, they refuse to be held accountable. Second, they don't always do a consistent job of holding their team members accountable. **Truth:** You'll never *willingly* choose accountability until your desire to change is greater than your fear of explaining your actions.

Stephen M. R. Covey and Rebecca R. Merrill put it this way in *The Speed Of Trust*: "Accountability builds extraordinary trust in the culture when people feel secure enough in the knowledge that everyone will be held accountable to certain standards. When leaders don't hold people accountable, the opposite is true. People feel it's unfair."

After participating in my yearlong mentoring program, Cliff Ourso, an agent in Donaldsonville, Louisiana, wrote me a testimonial letter. In part, it said: "Your ability to remind us of what we already know and then hold us accountable is what differentiates your program from others. The monthly conference calls keep us on track to reach our goals."

Ironically, when Cliff inquired about my mentoring program, I told him he didn't need it due to his long-term agency success. After working with him for a year, it became abundantly clear why Cliff enrolled in my program. Great agents know that accountability is necessary for continuous improvement and therefore, they welcome it.

Expectations Vs. Consequences

Great leaders link their expectations to consequences. What good does it do to set lofty annual expectations and not monitor your progress daily, weekly and monthly? In the case of Scott Foster's four aspirants—team members who want to become agents—they have to turn in daily activity reports. At a minimum, team members should account for their actions every week at the agency meeting.

"If a team member isn't living up to expectations," says David Wilcox, an agent in Gonzales, Louisiana, "I ask, 'How can I help you do better? What are you willing to change?' When I was a high school football coach, we graded every player and there were consequences. You were a champion, winner, 50-percenter or loser. At our agency, we grade on a whiteboard and it's kept daily by production lines. No one likes to be on the bottom. If you finish at the gold level, your commissions are higher."

Gale Breed, an agent in Lincoln, Nebraska, has a team leader named Garrett Schell. Garrett meets weekly with every other team member. Then, Gale does semiannual evaluations with each team member. "Prior to these evaluations, I've already met with Garrett and gone over the strengths and weaknesses of each team member."

Gale continues: "I'm searching for how my team members feel about what's going on in the agency and how we can get better. There's always a delicate balance between my expectations and how each team member goes about meeting these expectations. The key is to build relationships, reinforce what they're doing right and help them continue to grow."

Gale believes if you have team members who are bored with their daily activities, "you probably don't have the right people. I want highly self-motivated people serving our customers. Team energy and camaraderie are very important. A good work environment is critical. We try to make it fun with little contests and competition. The more engaged team members are, the less likely it is for boredom to occur. It all comes down to team members feeling a sense of ownership."

Terri Brock, an agent in Columbia, South Carolina, says: "Complacency is inevitable if there's no innate desire to learn and grow. We read a book entitled *Winning With Accountability* by Henry J. Evans. Here are two of his key points: (1) 'To front-load accountability into your organization, you have to provide crystal-clear expectations.' (2) 'Accountability is continuously asking: How am I doing?' It's a good read and less than a hundred pages."

It can be difficult to deal with team members who don't meet expectations. There must be consequences in order for accountability to be effective. This can range from additional training and mentoring, to warnings and even termination when it's clear that a team member is unwilling or incapable of reaching a certain production level.

Here are some of the excuses agents have shared for retaining underachieving team members too long:

- I don't have the heart to fire someone.
- I don't like confrontation.
- I dread looking for a replacement.
- I don't want to spend the time, money or effort to recruit new people.
- I've had this person on the team for several years.
- I don't want to start the training process all over again.
- I live in a small town and it's going to be awkward if I let this person go.
- I'd rather have a loyal, mediocre producer than a go-getter who may leave me soon.

As the leader of your agency, you have an obligation to your team to hire only the best people. **Fact:** Low performers will outlast everyone if you let them. Keep an accountability log and, sooner than later, help underperforming team members find more suitable careers. Make every effort to mentor middle performers until they become peak performers. Do everything possible to keep your superstars happy.

In *Courage To Lead*, Charlie Farrell offers this wise advice: "The most unpleasant thing you'll have to learn about leadership is discovering that everyone doesn't fit. You'll have to get rid of some people. And the quicker you do it, the less painful it will be."

Cooperation Vs. Confrontation

An agent once said, "Dick, accountability is my weakest area. I hate confrontation." No wonder this agent was struggling with accountability. Holding team members accountable shouldn't be adversarial. It's about gently reminding, not harshly rebuking. Most people will respond favorably to well-intentioned feedback and react defensively to scathing criticism.

Accountability should be a two-way street. If you expect to hold your team accountable, shouldn't you expect your team to hold you accountable? There's one major difference: you can terminate team members but they can't terminate you. Still, the goal of accountability should be a quest for excellence, agent included. No one should be above learning and growing.

"Accountability is personal," maintains Ray Cornprobst, a retired field leader in The Villages, Florida. "It starts with the agent setting the example. How can you expect the team to embrace accountability if you're not willing to embrace it? If team members feel like they have an ownership stake in the agency, they'll want to be held accountable—and not through micromanaging. In most cases, less is often more concerning accountability."

A Georgia field leader says: "A lot of agents don't like conflict. They don't like it when a team member points out their vulnerabilities. Agents need to understand that their teams are fully aware of any weaknesses they might have. It's no secret, so deal with them directly. Take ownership of your limitations. Welcome accountability as a way to improve continuously."

Stan Simmons, an agent in Lawrenceburg, Kentucky, says: "Accountability is one of the hardest and most complex issues in an agency. It's the difference between coasting and soaring. You have to inspect what you expect. I confess—this is an area I need to work on. The team is now evaluating my leadership twice a year. There's always room for improvement."

P. J. Johnson, an agent in North Charleston, South Carolina, sets the tone for cooperation and accountability when she hires someone. Every new employee signs a "customer service behaviors agreement":

Behaviors we promise to use when interacting with our customers:

- Smile and maintain positive eye contact.
- Offer a warm and sincere greeting to each and every customer. Use the customer's name when possible and introduce yourself.
- Offer assistance to customers, family members, other agent staff, claims and underwriting. Act first.
- Listen. When people complain, don't be defensive. Hear them out and show understanding. Give alternatives. Do what you can to make things right.
- Respond quickly. Say what you CAN do, not what you can't do.
- The team member who receives the complaint owns the complaint. Just because it isn't your job doesn't mean you can't help or find someone who can.

- Display appropriate body language at all times. Avoid talking about customers.
- Escort customers to offices rather than pointing.
- Create a positive work environment. Practice teamwork. Respect and support your fellow team members.
- Be an ambassador for our agency in and outside the workplace.
- Answer the customer's inquiries by being knowledgeable about our agency and products.
- Use proper telephone etiquette. Answer within three rings and with a "smile"; ask permission to put a caller on hold. Eliminate transfer when possible.
- Picking up trash and maintaining the cleanliness of our agency office area and surrounding grounds is the responsibility of every team member.
- Maintain a professional image. You are part of a proud agency team. Look the part.

Team Member Promise: By signing, I acknowledge that I have read and understand the expectations for service behaviors. I agree to abide by these behaviors and understand that failure to do so can be grounds for termination.

Team Member: _____ Agent: _____
Date: _____

Growth Vs. Stagnation

In thinking about the connection between growth and accountability, I remember a story of a father and his fifteen-year-old son. The father was having difficulty holding his son accountable in two major areas—school and his bedroom. Johnny's grades were abysmal and his room was always in disarray. Despite the father's persistence, nothing seemed to change with his son.

One day the father passed by Johnny's bedroom expecting to see the usual mess—unmade bed, a pile of dirty clothes on the floor and empty soft drink cans strewn everywhere. Incredibly, his son's bedroom was immaculate. Walking in to get a closer look at this rare sight, the father noticed an envelope leaning against a pillow. It was addressed "Dear Dad." He opened it quickly and began to read:

Dear Dad:

It's with regret and sorrow that I'm writing you. I had to elope with my new girlfriend because I wanted to avoid a scene with you and Mom. I've been finding real passion with Stacy, and she is so nice. But I knew you wouldn't approve of her because of all her piercings, her tattoos, her tight motorcycle pants and the fact that she's much older than I am.

Please understand that it's not only the passion, Dad. Stacy is pregnant and says we'll be very happy. She owns a trailer in the woods and has a stack of firewood for the entire winter. We share a dream of having many more children. Stacy has opened my eyes to the fact that marijuana doesn't really hurt anyone.

In the meantime, we're praying that science will find a cure for AIDS so Stacy can get better. She deserves it. So don't worry, Dad, I'm fifteen and I know how to take care of myself. I'm sure we'll be back some day to visit so you can get to know your grandchildren.

Love, Johnny

P. S.

Dad, none of the above is true. I'm over at Tommy's house. I just wanted to remind you that there are worse things in life than a report card, which you'll find in the center drawer of my desk. I love you. Call me when it's safe to come home!

Johnny's father still wasn't pleased with his son's grades, but at least progress was being made in the boy's room. Isn't it often this way with some team members? You have to persist until you get the results you're seeking. Just as that father understood the correlation between accountability and optimal growth for his son, it's also true for great agents and their team members. Growth and accountability should be as inseparable as a boy and his dog.

Jon Gordon says this in *Training Camp:* "If you are always striving to get better, then you are always growing. And if you are growing, then you are not comfortable." Languishing in a comfort zone isn't good for you, the team or your customers. It leads to stagnation and complacency.

Boyd Bailey, founder of Wisdom Hunters LLC, provides this sage advice: "Complacency is a killer because it doesn't care. It kills outcomes because it doesn't care about excellent execution. It kills relationships because it doesn't care about investing in the good of another. It kills finances because it doesn't care if spending drifts into irresponsible expenditures. It kills life because it doesn't care if lethargic living leads to premature death."

To shun complacency, avoid stagnation and grow your agency, here's a **SIMPLE** accountability system to consider:

- **S**et expectations. What goals do you want to achieve during the year? Are they included in your annual business plan and does everyone have a copy?
- **I**nvite commitment. Are your team members really serious about reaching their goals? What incentives are in place for the team to reach its goals?
- **M**onitor progress. How are the team members doing in pursuit of their goals? Are you asking everyone to give progress reports at the weekly agency meetings?
- **P**rovide feedback. What are you doing to help your team members reach their goals? How are they responding to your advice?
- **L**ink to consequences. What is the outcome when team members don't reach their goals? Have your team members truly embraced the need for accountability?
- **E**valuate effectiveness. When team members reach their goals, how are you recognizing and celebrating these achievements? When goals aren't reached, what happened and how can you help your team members be more successful in subsequent years?

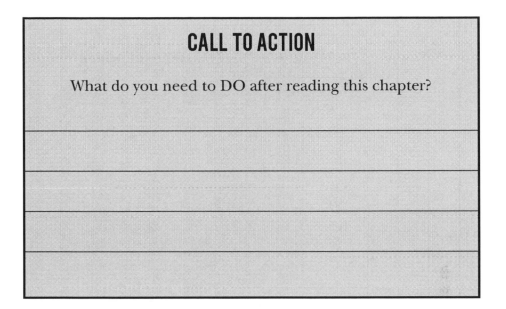

Chapter 20:
MULTIPLYING YOUR INFLUENCE

"A teacher affects eternity; he can never tell
where his influence stops."
–Henry Adams, *The Education Of Henry Adams*

Theme:
Are you instilling an entrepreneurial spirit within your team?

Key Points:
- Leading by example
- Helping team members become leaders
- Offering a path for team members to become agents

Scotty Cole and I met when he was a first-grader. He was my protégé in the mentoring program at a nearby school. When the counselor called to tell me about Scotty, she said he was repeating the first grade. His parents were divorced and he had some behavior problems due to his poor vision. What really got my attention, though, was when the counselor said, "Scotty is a real sweet boy, but he needs to work on his self-confidence."

This old marine sergeant devised a simple plan to help Scotty become more confident. Every week we'd have the following exchange during our hour together at the school:

Dick: What are goals?
Scotty: Goals are things you want to do and places you want to go.

Dick: That's right. And what is confidence?
Scotty: Confidence means you can do something.
Dick: And what will negative people tell you?
Scotty: They'll say I can't do it.
Dick: So what do you say to these people?
Scotty: I can do it—unless it's something stupid or bad!

Every September, we established three goals at school and three goals at home. We repeated this format year after year. I monitored the progress of his goals and when Scotty succeeded in reaching them, we celebrated. When he failed to reach a certain goal, we talked about what could be done to make him successful.

Hopefully, I had a good influence on Scotty during our twelve years together. One of my proudest moments was watching this young man graduate from high school in 2012. He wasn't an honor student, but the kid didn't quit and received his diploma. Best of all, Scotty stayed out of trouble during his school years by choosing his friends wisely. He's now working full-time in the restaurant business and doing well.

Leading By Example

As an agency leader, you have a profound influence on your team members. They tend to follow your example. Influence is a two-edged sword. If you're positive, the team will probably be positive. If you're negative, the team is likely to be negative. What example are you setting?

Tom Wright, an agent in Porterville, California, shared a powerful story to illustrate the value of associating with positive people. "My buddy and I were a couple miles out in the Pacific Ocean fishing for halibut. We received a call from the harbor master saying we should come ashore. There was a concern about a tsunami because unusual currents were pulling water out of the port. Suddenly, a twenty-five-foot wave came right at us. My partner turned the boat sharply at the last minute and we just missed that giant wave. We would have died without quick action."

Tom's lesson learned: "Flee trouble or bad things will happen to you. Similarly, hanging around negative people isn't a healthy environment. I've always tried to swim downstream with the company I represent by doing what they ask. A lot of agents complain about things that are out of our control. They're mad all the time. They're bitter. I want to set a positive example to my team each day. It's more difficult to do if you're hanging around negative people."

"I serve my team the same way I do my customers," declares Bill Kolb, an agent in Pryor, Oklahoma. "I like to ask, 'What can I do for you?' My role is to be their cheerleader. I don't have all the answers, but collectively we do. My team is on the front line getting shot at. I'm the general in the rear supplying whatever they need to be successful. Give the credit away. I brag on my team members in front of customers. I accept any awards on behalf of the team. Excessive ego can ruin your agency. We can't reach our full potential if it's all about me."

Bill continues: "A lot of agents complain about things not being the way they used to be. I tell them we'd be in trouble if this was the case. I ask, 'When was the business the most fun?' They usually say it was when they first started their agencies. I tell them to make it fun and challenging again by getting back to the basics, including leadership by example. If an agent isn't happy, the team won't be happy. So much of leadership is attitude and the mirror image you project to your team."

What do you see when you look in that mirror? Are you leading by example or abdication? To influence your team members at a higher level, ask these questions:

- Do they trust me?
- Do they feel I understand their needs?
- Do they know I care about their welfare?
- Do they feel comfortable around me?
- Do they listen when I communicate?
- Do they comprehend what I share?
- Do they believe what I say?
- Do they remember my messages?
- Do they act on my desires?

Helping Team Members Become Leaders

Influence is about multiplication, not addition. You'll be a more successful leader if you understand this principle. For example, if I give you a penny a day for one month, you'll have thirty cents. However, if I give you a penny the first day, double that amount the second day, and continue this pattern for the next thirty days, you'll have nearly $5.4 million in a month. If you're in doubt, do the math; multiplication beats addition every time.

Imagine what would happen if you applied this multiplication principle to your agency. Instead of looking for team members to do a specific job, why not challenge them to take on certain leadership responsibilities as well? You'll get a better return on your investment if you do.

Mark King has been a team member at Scott Foster's agency for ten years. Mark's official title is "financial services representative," but he does so much more. In addition to selling life insurance, long-term care insurance and mutual funds, Mark helps coach Scott's four aspirants, assists with the agency's role-playing activities, leads the monthly long-term care workshop and acts as a sounding board to the team to keep Scott from being overwhelmed by things he shouldn't be doing.

"One of Scott's greatest strengths," says Mark, "is that he recognizes talents in people and encourages leadership. He really appreciates team members who step forward and take on added responsibility. If there's something that will help the agency, Scott will appoint a go-to person to take charge of this project and empower them to make decisions. From time to time, he'll ask one of his aspirants to run our team meetings."

Tom McQueeney, an agent in Charleston, South Carolina, states: "Throughout my career, I've noticed that once someone moves on—I've had five team members go into agency—another person rises to a new level. It's truly amazing how a junior team member takes charge and thrives almost immediately."

Tom continues: "We seem to depend on the top person without really focusing on giving new responsibilities to less experienced team members. More times than not, they want the added responsibility because it edifies their importance to the agency. Agents need to recognize and embrace the fact that team members want to have value beyond a paycheck."

Cliff Ourso, an agent in Donaldsonville, Louisiana, believes in helping team members become leaders. "I give them the authority and responsibility to make decisions. This ship is too big to micromanage. If something is wrong, we'll fix it. My team members know they can bring problems to me, but only if they have three solutions. Of course, if a team member has the answers to a certain problem, why does he or she need to come to me anyway?"

A Georgia field leader says: "Agents should treat their team members like all-stars. This means trusting them. This means giving up some of your authority so they can take on certain leadership roles within the agency. This means allowing them to make some mistakes. This means being a great listening post. Don't expect team members to believe what you're asking them to do if you don't believe it. Take a hard look at how you're communicating to your team."

Offering A Path For Team Members To Become Agents

Scott Foster participates in something called an aspirant program. He recruits at college campuses and seeks team members who want to become agents. They work for Scott as salespeople for a three-year period. Aspirants are paid a base monthly salary of $1,500–$2,000, plus commissions and bonuses. There are no guarantees but at the end of this trial period, Scott recommends aspirants for agency school.

Scott gets bright college graduates who are highly self-motivated to succeed in the insurance and financial services profession. Aspirants get an opportunity for a direct path to agency and a lucrative career. The agency benefits with increased production and profitability. Scott has three "graduates" who are now agents, and four aspirants—Scott Cross, Luke Darch, Brett Moore and Carlisle Whitley—who are on track to become agents.

The Scott Foster Agency aspirant program is very structured. Every aspect of this training is recorded on a "recognition checklist," which includes dates of hiring and licensing; a wide range of skill checks from product knowledge and role-playing, to sales training and customer relations; and a host of other administrative activities designed to prepare the aspirant for agency.

Here's an inspiring letter Scott wrote to his aspirants:

You've been given an opportunity—an opportunity to earn money for you and your family, an opportunity to learn and grow, an opportunity for a career. But when did it change from an opportunity you GET to do to an obligation you've GOT to do?

Let's examine what it takes to have a successful sales career. You have to make a lot of calls. You have to follow up on these calls. You have to have appointments to learn about the needs of your prospects and customers. After identifying certain needs, you have to make sales. These are challenging activities but if they weren't difficult, everyone would be trying to do what you do.

As a result, these challenges should change your attitude from "I've GOT to make these calls" to "I GET to do this opportunity." Perhaps your attitude changes so slowly that it's imperceptible, but it does change whether you want to be successful. Therefore, why not change one simple letter in the way you think? Instead of using an "O" as in "I've GOT to do this," why not use an "E" as in "I GET to do this? The letter E could also stand for enthusiasm, excitement and excellence. Wouldn't that make your daily task a lot more palatable?

Another proponent of the aspirant program is Scott Garvey, an agent in Baltimore, Maryland. Scott has eight young salespeople who want to become agents. "They have to pay for all of their licensing fees before joining the agency—an investment of perhaps $700. I want to find out if they're willing to bear some of the risk of becoming an entrepreneur. Once they're on board, I reimburse their investment. I tell them it costs up to $200,000 to become a medical doctor, but this is an even better opportunity."

Scott has a very methodical, intentional training program. Each aspirant receives a *Playbook* focused on purpose, values and agency culture. "I expect them to be active learners. They have to spend time with a service team member to understand the consequences of doing something improperly and how it impacts our customers. They spend time with a more experienced aspirant. I expect them to be doing two hundred quotes and producing sixty apps per month after three months at the agency."

Scott continues: "I don't train the team. The team trains the team. I do sit with each aspirant about once a month and ask, 'What do you need from me to be successful?' I want them to reject passivity, accept responsibility and develop the mind-set of a champion. It's hard work for the aspirants but a labor of love for me. There's nothing more enjoyable than pouring yourself into the lives of these young people and seeing them succeed. What I'm doing is creating a pipeline of future agents for the company I represent."

If you're intimidated by the idea of launching an aspirant program at your agency, follow this advice from speaker Patricia Fripp: "Think big; start small." Seek the counsel of other agents who've implemented this program. Visit a favorite university and introduce the idea to the proper officials, who'll probably love it. Talk to executives at the company(s) you represent to glean their insights. After doing your homework, make a plan and take action. If you can't get excited about multiplying your influence, why are you leading?

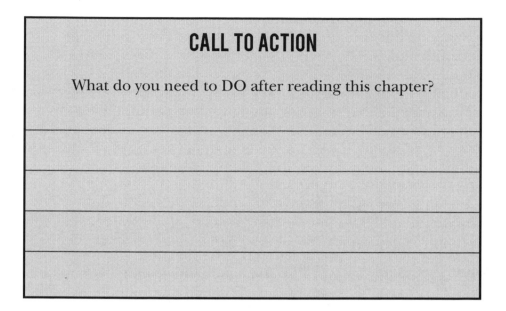

CALL TO ACTION

What do you need to DO after reading this chapter?

TIER 5:
THE TREASURED LEADER

It's about a legacy and inspirational impact

Maturing Through Change

Focusing On Fiscal Fitness

Striving For Work/Life Balance

Leaving A Legitimate Leadership Legacy

Crossing The Greatest Gap In Life

Chapter 21:
MATURING THROUGH CHANGE

"The pain of every change is forgotten when the benefits of that change are realized."
–Tom Hopkins, *How To Master The Art Of Selling*

Theme:
Are you living in the past or concentrating more on today and a bright future?

Key Points:
- Facts about change
- Familiar reasons for avoiding change and growth
- The headache of changing or the heartache of not changing

Dr. Ignaz Phillip Semmelweis was a legendary change master. He stepped out of his comfort zone, took a huge risk and changed the medical field forever. Born in 1818, this Hungarian gynecologist had an impact on medical history that's felt every day in hospitals around the world. We owe a big debt of gratitude to a man who had the courage of his convictions, a hero willing to implement a new and better idea.

It's hard to believe now, but one out of eight mothers died from childbirth fever in the mid-nineteenth century. While serving at the renowned Vienna General Hospital in Austria, Dr. Semmelweis observed as physicians performed autopsies and then, without washing their hands, examined expectant mothers. Dr. Jakob

Kolletschka, his closest friend, died shortly after cutting his finger while performing an autopsy.

Dr. Semmelweis was the first to associate such examinations with infection and death. He used a chlorine solution and lost one mother in fifty after delivering 8,537 babies in eleven years. His findings were published in *The Etiology, Concept & Prophylaxis Of Childbirth Fever.* Most doctors ignored this book.

Because he knew his procedure was right, Dr. Semmelweis refused to give up. He spent hours lecturing on this simple procedure and debating with his colleagues. He pleaded with them to change, but his efforts were met with fierce resistance and ridicule. Dr. Semmelweis wrote in frustration:

"Puerperal (childbirth) fever is caused by decomposed material conveyed to a wound. I have shown how it can be prevented. I have proven all that I have said. But while we talk, talk, talk, gentlemen, women are dying. I'm not asking anything world-shaking. I'm only asking that you wash—for God's sake, wash your hands!"

Dr. Semmelweis spent the best years of his short life trying to convince the medical profession to change. His crusade led to mental illness, insanity and death at the age of forty-seven. His associates were probably laughing in his face while thousands of pregnant women died because doctors were too proud to wash their hands.

In 1865, the year of Semmelweis's death, Dr. Joseph Lister performed his first antiseptic operation. It was soon acknowledged that Dr. Semmelweis had been right. This brave change master is known as the "father of infection control." He's honored by an Edouard Chassaing sculpture standing in the Hall Of Medical Immortals in Chicago, Illinois.

Facts About Change

Are you mastered by change, or are you a change master? Are you in a deep hole and still digging? Do you find yourself saying, "I've always done things this way…I dread learning a new system…I wish these changes would just go away." Or do you get excited about new ways to do old things? Do you welcome opportunities to learn and grow?

The pace and volume of change in today's business environment is staggering. You can complain about all of the changes, but your competition couldn't care less if you change—and hopes you don't. However, you can't grow if you don't change, and if you don't grow, how can you possibly deal with the high expectations of today's demanding customers?

Elaine Scott, women's group director at Browns Bridge Community Church and Gwinnett Church in metro Atlanta, says: "Growth is that inconvenient space between where you are and where you want to be. Expect to have growing pains during the journey."

Steve Cannon, an agent in Woodstock, Georgia, says: "We can't control a lot of the changes in our profession. However, at our agency, we aren't going to allow the economy to control what we do. We're a sales organization, so we're going to sell. It's how we grow. When other agents call to complain about rates, underwriting and other things beyond our control, I don't have time for that."

Here are four aspects of change to consider:

No change is impossible. Do you know that you could "head for the hills," completely abandon society, and you'd still change? You'd have to change the way you find food and shelter. Your appearance would certainly change. You'd have to change how you spend your time. You'd get older and, well, you get the idea.

Trying to avoid change is like trying to avoid breathing—and both are deadly. It's no different with your agency. You simply can't ignore change without severe consequences. The choice is simple: complain about change and go the way of the dinosaur, or change and continue to evolve as a business owner.

Some change is impractical. The Ten Commandments are so fundamentally true that they've never been edited. Would you say that it's OK to lie to your employer, but it's not OK to lie to your parents? Lying is lying. Not even an atheist wants to be lied to, stolen from or murdered! Another example is the US Constitution, which is so solid that it has only been amended twenty-seven times since 1787. Indeed, the American founding fathers were wise leaders.

The same is true with your agency values and purpose. These guiding standards should remain constant throughout your career. There will always be a place for core values such as integrity, honesty, humility, loyalty, respect and teamwork—and for purposeful agencies dedicated to helping customers with their insurance and financial services needs.

Most change is painful. As a runner for nearly fifty years, I'm always taken aback when people quit exercising after a week or two because they're sore, tired or lethargic. Going from sedentary and overweight to fit and trim is painful. The key is to focus on the long-term gain instead of the short-term pain.

It's no different with complacent agents. Making major changes is uncomfortable and comes with growing pains. However, it sure beats the alternative—remaining stagnant, losing business and not reaching your full potential.

Every change has consequences. Al Clark, an agent in Arlington, Texas, moved from Minnesota to Texas to start a scratch agency in

1979. In *Al Clark's Multi-Million Dollar Formula 4 Success,* he says: "I started with no customers, no policies and no income. I've been whatever size you are right now."

Al has made countless changes over the years to remain competitive, but his core values and purpose have stayed constant. The consequences have been remarkable. Al has been the number one agent eighteen times for the insurance company he represents. I love his business philosophy: ability plus attitude plus activity minus excuses equals success.

Of course, it's also true that refusing to change produces consequences. What about the consequences of complacency, procrastination, low expectations and uninspired leadership? What about the consequences of avoiding wise counsel, dismissing ongoing education, failing to see the big picture and leaving a mediocre legacy? If any of these consequences are nagging at you, it's never too late to change.

Familiar Reasons For Avoiding Change And Growth

A veteran agent said after a seminar: "Dick, I love your ideas. You're informative, inspiring, relevant and challenging. Unfortunately, two of my agent friends missed what you had to say today. Now, please don't take it personally. They don't attend *any* meetings. They're mad because of all the changes that have occurred in recent years."

Change is a source of torment for many agents. But since change is inevitable, you're either resisting it or embracing it. Your choice can make you bitter or better. Bitterness erodes your attitude, health and productivity. Bitterness jeopardizes agency growth. Bitterness, if unchecked, can lead to disillusionment, depression, despair and destruction.

Betterment requires a constant monitoring of your mind-set. Betterment demands a long-term commitment to ongoing learning. Betterment is how your dreams become deeds and your deeds become your destiny. Are you bitter or better?

If you're not sure how to change directions, surround yourself with positive agents and mentors who are willing to help you get from where you are to where you could be. Most importantly, stop hanging around negative people, having pity parties and longing for the "good old days." This counterproductive activity is a waste of your valuable time and energy.

Here are some of the reasons agents have shared for resisting change and refusing to grow:

- I have no desire to get out of my comfort zone.
- I like the freedom of owning a small agency.
- I was hired to be a salesperson, not a leader.
- I tried expanding and lost a lot of money.
- I don't want the headaches of leading a bigger team.
- I don't have room to add more people at my current location.
- I don't want to spend the time needed to train a team of specialists.
- I don't want to work any harder than I already do.
- I'm already making a lucrative income.

In talking with producers at all levels over the years, I have found there are four broad types of agents. This information is shared not to be judgmental but rather to help you assess what type of agent you are, determine if any changes need to be made and take any necessary action:

Traditionalist—This agent says: I'm going to keep doing what I've always done. I was hired to sell a couple of products, and that's what I'm going to do until retirement. I'm already making a comfortable living, so there's no need to change.

Idealist—This agent says: I'll start offering other products when I'm more knowledgeable, the timing is better, my team is bigger and better trained, the competition forces me to change and so on. But I just don't see the urgency to act now and I'm holding off.

Experimentalist—This agent says: I'm still not sure about offering more products, adding new team members and doing what it takes to educate our customers about additional risks. However, I'm going to test out this new approach for a few months and see what happens.

Evolutionist—This agent says: I'll build a team of peak-performing specialists. It'll require a fundamental shift in my thinking, a daring financial investment and, initially, more of my time. Still, I see this as a challenging, profitable opportunity and I'm 100 percent committed.

The Headache Of Changing Or The Heartache Of Not Changing

This chapter subtitle is the name of one of my keynote talks. The idea is that most change is a headache but refusing to change can produce a more painful heartache. For example, it can be a headache to hire new team members. However, if this process is ignored, the heartache is often a stagnant agency unwilling to embrace change in the critical area of human resources.

Perhaps you remember the old television commercial by Fram, a purveyor of vehicle oil filters: "You can pay me now or you can pay me later." If you fail to change your oil filter right away, you might not notice any immediate difference. So you continue driving a car with a two-year-old oil filter while sludge builds up gradually in the engine. When it finally dies, the cost of a new engine is much greater than that of an inexpensive oil filter.

Perhaps nothing will teach you more about mastering change than your life's turning points. A turning point is a "time in which a significant change occurs." Most people experience three to nine turning points in life, depending upon how they live and how long they live.

These major changes can begin positively—graduating from college, getting married, securing that first job or having children. Or these changes can begin negatively—suffering a major financial loss, battling a health challenge, losing a loved one or getting divorced. Regardless of how a turning point begins, you can gain valuable perspective by learning from these transitional times and growing at a deeper level over time.

I often ask agents to do the following exercise. Take out a blank piece of paper and write these three categories across the top of the page: year, turning point and impact. List the year each turning began, what the turning points were and, if enough time has elapsed to provide perspective, what the long-term impact was:

Year	Turning Point	Impact
————	————————————	————————————
————	————————————	————————————
————	————————————	————————————
————	————————————	————————————
————	————————————	————————————
————	————————————	————————————
————	————————————	————————————
————	————————————	————————————
————	————————————	————————————
————	————————————	————————————
————	————————————	————————————
————	————————————	————————————
————	————————————	————————————

For example, my biggest turning point occurred in 1982 when I met Judy on December 15. In retrospect, the long-term impact has been enormous. We were married on August 4, 1984. I became a stepfather to Rebecca and Tara, who were fifteen and twelve respectively. Eventually, I became a grandfather to Jackson, who is now thirteen. I've enjoyed many wonderful years with Judy. We've also experienced some trying times in virtually every area of our lives, but we've persevered together as a team for more than three decades.

Scott Garvey, an agent in Baltimore, Maryland, knows how stressful a turning point can be. "After a couple of team members became agents, I got a little lazy and took my eye off the ball. I didn't replace these two people with capable substitutes and production dipped. I had no passion and didn't enjoy coming to the office. I hired an office manager and abdicated the leadership of my agency to this person. Revenues dropped and I had to pull my five kids out of a private Christian school because I couldn't afford the tuition."

Scott goes on: "I call this period in my life the 'Walk Of Shame.' Of course, if I hadn't gotten so low, I probably wouldn't have changed. Reluctantly, I went to a study club meeting and the guest speaker's message resonated. That's when I decided to start my agency aspirant program for team members who want to become agents. The thing I enjoy most about my career is developing young people who are the future agents of the company I represent."

So much of being willing to change is associated with your attitude. Typically, resistance to change is the focus of gripe sessions with other agents. I'm not saying you shouldn't speak up about situations that need changing. However, if complaining is your daily mode of operation, you're going about things the wrong way. How often have you felt better after a gripe session?

In today's rapidly changing business environment, it's easy to dwell on a time when things were simpler and slower paced. But since the past is gone forever, how productive is it to concentrate on what used to be? Worst of all, your obsession with the past is probably interfering with a wealth of opportunities today and in the future.

Jim Cornwell, an agent in Tampa, Florida, makes this observation. "I've seen a lot of good agents that can't make the necessary changes. They whine. They get bitter. It's sad. This was particularly true when we lost the ability to write homeowner's insurance after suffering four hurricanes in one year. Bitterness just eats you up. You have to adapt, embrace change and move on because some things are beyond our control."

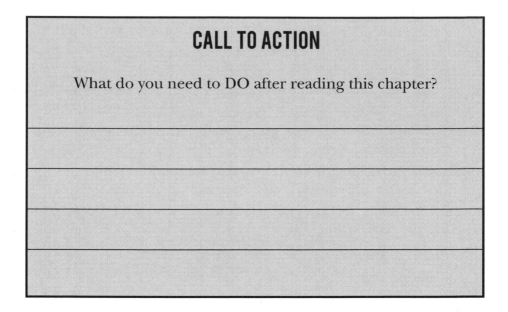

CALL TO ACTION

What do you need to DO after reading this chapter?

Chapter 22:
FOCUSING ON FISCAL FITNESS

"You must gain control over your money or the lack of it will
forever control you."
–Dave Ramsey, *Total Money Makeover*

Theme:
Do you have financial peace about your agency investment?

Key Points:
- It takes a team
- It takes toil
- It takes time

I spent thirteen years in sales and sales management, with virtually all of my income earned through commissions and bonuses.
I've been a small business owner since 1982. If there's no monthly
production, I don't get paid. Knowing what I know now—and provided it was possible to return to my twenties—I'd probably be an
insurance agent. It has a lot to do with your compensation plan.

You get generous first-year commissions. Some of you earn hefty
annual bonuses for exceptional production. You get renewal income even if you have a bad month or year. You have the opportunity to save a lot of money. While it's not available to the agents who
were interviewed for this book, some of you can sell your agencies
at retirement and realize a nice windfall. If you've invested in your

own building, you can eventually sell or rent it. Why would you ever complain about such a pay plan?

This is probably the shortest chapter in the book, but it might be the most important one for some of you. Money certainly isn't everything, but it can definitely disrupt your way of life when finances aren't managed wisely. On the other hand, if you produce consistently, monitor overhead closely and invest carefully, you can enjoy a financial peace of mind that most people only dream about.

It Takes A Team

Gale Breed, an agent in Lincoln, Nebraska, says: "The best investment you can make is in your team, but I didn't always feel this way. I was making more money in the stock market than I was as an agent before 9/11. When the stock market crashed after that horrendous event, I lost a lot of money. It led to a big turning point in my career. Ironically, I didn't know that much about the stock market, which was totally out of my control. I decided to invest in something within my control. I increased the size of my team and moved into a larger facility within a few years."

Gale continues: "What holds so many agents back is worrying that if they spend a dollar, they have to get in back. It doesn't always work that way. It's part of being an entrepreneur. You have to be brave and disciplined. You have to accept some failure. So often agents spend excessively on new cars, rental properties, vacations and other things instead of investing a certain percentage of their profits back into the business and hiring more team members.

"For example, let's say an agency is grossing $500,000 per year and netting $250,000 after overhead and taxes. Instead of the agent taking out all of the profit and spending it on personal things, why not set aside a percentage to allow for fluctuating income and a percentage for marketing and hiring new team members? It's this kind of long-term commitment that will help you grow your agency *and* provide fiscal peace of mind. It sounds simple, but it's done rarely."

Tony Pope, an agent with locations in Summerville and Mount Pleasant, South Carolina, agrees. "You have to reinvest in your agency. If you're going to spend, why not put your money into people? I have twenty team members and we haven't had much turnover."

Tony continues: "Many agents say they can't afford to hire more people, but can you afford not to? Growing my market share is the least I can do for the company I represent. The best way to grow is with people who love working for you. I don't want this to sound egotistical, but we have an enjoyable place to work."

It Takes Toil

Scott Foster says you must plan to work hard if you want to enjoy long-term financial success. "Be involved with your team. Train your people, which is the one of the best investments you can make. Do your best to avoid debt. Buy as much whole life insurance as you can afford. Try not to let your overhead, including taxes, exceed more than 50 percent of your gross revenue."

Al Clark, a perennial top-ten agent in Arlington, Texas, is married to Shalyn, another top-ten producer in Hurst, Texas: "We've worked hard so we could retire at fifty-five if we chose to. We're still working because we want to, not because we have to. Since we have two household incomes, we try to live on one. We stay within our means and don't overspend. The key is to have a plan and be consistent and disciplined in executing it. If you're giving financial advice to your customers, shouldn't you have your own affairs in order?"

Besides being a great agent, Al is also a brilliant businessman. He created four exhaustive manuals covering every aspect of agency operations. In *Al Clark's Multi-Million Dollar Formula 4 Success*, he gives these money management recommendations:

- Have no consumer debt except for home mortgage.
- Have no car loans.
- Have no credit card debt.
- Save a minimum of 10 percent of your income.
- Take the minimum cash out of your agency, especially in the early years.
- Own your own property and building.
- Keep the salaries of salespeople low and bonuses high.

It Takes Time

"It takes time to be profitable," says Scott Foster. "Set realistic expectations. Make sure your family is on board with the time table for when you'll start making money. Be prepared to invest money in the first three to five years, especially on good people. Realize that this front-end outlay will produce a long-term return on your investment. For example, I bought an office building early in my career and rented it out for years to pay the mortgage and earn some extra income. It's now paid for and completely occupied by our team."

"So often," says Don Rood Jr., a field leader in Los Angeles, California, "agents don't take the long-term view. A lot of their annual revenue is going to overhead, including an affluent lifestyle. They don't have enough money to reinvest in their business. They're stuck. They're trapped. Most of all, agency growth is dead."

Don continues: "Agents need to think about where the money is going. They need to concentrate more on delayed gratification, not instant gratification. They need to understand what they're building toward and have some cushion. Sometimes, when the profits start rolling in, they lose all common sense. If you pull too much money out to live on early in your career, you'll limit your growth later on."

Patrick Morley provides an interesting perspective on financial peace in *The Seven Seasons Of A Man's Life:* "Poverty and prosperity are both great tests but, biblically speaking, prosperity is the greater test. Poverty risks the body, but prosperity risks the soul. All the benefits of money are temporal, while all the risks of money are eternal."

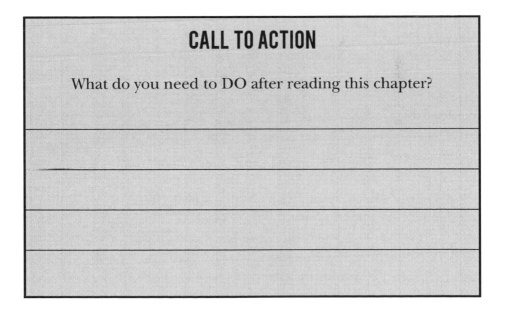

CALL TO ACTION

What do you need to DO after reading this chapter?

Chapter 23:

STRIVING FOR WORK/LIFE BALANCE

"A cheerful heart is good medicine, but a broken
spirit saps a person's strength."
–Proverbs 17:22 (NLT)

Theme:
Are you burning brightly or burning out?

Key Points:
- Perfect balance is a myth
- Burnout is optional
- Manage stress by making time for serenity

After thirteen years in sales and sales management, I quit a lucrative career and didn't work for five months in 1982. I was a
burned-out workaholic. I appeared happy on the outside because,
after all, I possessed many so-called tangibles of success. On the
inside, though, I was miserable. I was living an incredibly unbalanced life focused on me, money, materialism, merriment and
mega-hours at work.

My self-imposed sabbatical was a time of stress and serenity. Naturally, I was concerned about my next career, but I loved the peaceful time off. Two major events changed everything. Within a ten-
week period in the last quarter of 1982, I started my company and
met Judy, who became my wife two years later. Entrepreneurship
helped me realize that there's more to career satisfaction than

making money. Judy was the catalyst in a return to the spiritual foundation of my upbringing. I went from success to significance.

For nineteen frustrating years, I lived an unbalanced lifestyle based on *have > think > do > be*. I was driven by the *haves* of a materialistic world. This quest influenced my *thinking* and *doing*. I failed to *be* true to myself, others and God.

Since 1982, I've endeavored to live a more balanced life based on *be > think > do > have*. I strive to *be* faithful to Biblical truths. This way of life has influenced my *thinking* and *doing*. My *haves* now extend far beyond material things to intangible blessings.

There's nothing wrong with having nice possessions, money in the bank, professional success and fun times. I enjoy all of these things. However, when these tangibles were the center of my life, I had a broken spirit. Now, I have a cheerful heart, for I'm burning brightly in the spiritual, mental, physical and emotional realms of my life.

Adopting a more balanced lifestyle doesn't mean there won't be struggles. I continue to experience my share of difficult challenges, and so will you. We walk a fine line between failure and success, sadness and happiness, unbalanced and balanced living. Channing Pollock said it well: "Happiness is a weigh station between too little and too much."

Perfect Balance Is A Myth

There's no such thing as a perfectly balanced life *every* day. Sure, there are those seemingly perfect days when you're around everything you love. You exercise and have some quiet time with God early in the morning. You have a productive day at the office, including lunch with your good friends at the civic club. You get home in time for dinner with your family. The day's mail includes an unexpected refund check and big bump in your portfolio. You spend the evening watching a movie with some neighbors. Sounds like heaven on earth, right?

In the real world, life doesn't always go so dreamingly. The quest for *perfect* balance is a myth. There are days when work is all-consuming. There are days when you're tending to sick or dying loved ones. There are days when you're on vacation and simply having fun. There are days when you're volunteering in the community and don't get home until late. There are days when you're at your attorney's office dealing with personal or business affairs. There are days when you're at a spiritual retreat trying to focus on God and his will for your life.

This doesn't mean you shouldn't pursue a reasonable work/life balance. But balancing the work you do with the life you lead is easier said than done. The following tool has helped me be more on-purpose in my life and business. Perhaps you'll find it useful as well:

The Master Plan Funnel Concept

Purpose
(Lifetime Meaning)
Why am I here?

Dominant Interests
(Focus)
Where do I spend my time?

Goals
(Short & Long-Term Motivation)
Where am I going?

Priorities
(Daily Results)
What will I do
today?

It works like this: When priorities get done daily, goals are eventually realized. When goals are achieved in all of your dominant interests, there is balance. When there is balance, you're more likely to fulfill your purpose and lead a more meaningful life personally and professionally.

Purpose, goals and priorities are covered elsewhere in these pages, so let's examine dominant interests. These are the really important areas where you spend time. Personally, this could include family, friends, community, place of worship, physical fitness and so on. Professionally, this could include sales, marketing, finances, administration, service, leadership development, team training, community outreach and more.

Most people have three to seven dominant interests in their personal lives, and perhaps three to five at work. For example, my dominant interests are God, others (family, friends and community) and personal (health/leisure, business and finances). Breaking down the business side, my dominant interests are the messenger (my spiritual, mental, physical and emotional well-being), message (topics), marketing (clients) and management (everything else).

Once identified, it's critical to spend an appropriate but not equal amount of time in each dominant interest, knowing that it might be daily, weekly or less often depending upon what's happening in your life at a particular time. For example, you probably spend a lot more time working and being with your family than you do exercising and going to church. **Caution:** If you say it's a dominant interest and you don't spend any time there, is it really an important part of your life?

Scott Garvey, an agent in Baltimore, Maryland, says: "I struggle with work/life balance. I work a full week. So when I'm at the agency, I often feel like I'm cheating my family. And when I'm with my family, I sometimes feel like I'm cheating my agency. I'm getting ready to open another location, which is going to be a challenging balancing act."

"You can have all the success in the world," maintains Kirk Baker, an agent in Valencia, California, "but it shouldn't come by neglecting your family. One of the ways I overcome this struggle is by taking my family on the award trips we earn by reaching certain production levels. This is something the kids will always remember. In my four areas of importance—spiritual, family, business and health—I believe life is better with balance. I try not to sacrifice one for the other."

Burnout Is Optional

Perhaps you feel like you're on a business battlefield at times. If you're not careful, the pressures of the insurance and financial services profession can lead to a workaholic lifestyle and burnout. It's good to work hard, but it's counterproductive to work all the time. Be grateful for your workplace family, but remember to make time for the other key relationships in your life—spouse, children, relatives, friends, mentors and your Heavenly Father.

"Most people rust out before they burn out," declares Ray Cornprobst, a retired field leader in The Villages, Florida. "They get stale, bored and complacent. They don't change with the times and they long for the 'good old days.' It becomes a joyless job instead of an exciting career. You not only have to 'smell the roses,' but you also have to grow fresh new roses. This often means working smarter, not harder. You can't be what you want to be by being what you've been."

Sam Eubank, a field leader in Newburgh, New York, makes an interesting observation: "In recruiting new team members, agents should stress how they can provide flexibility that might not be possible at a bigger company. You can't place a value on certain benefits. That's the beauty of working at a small business like an agency. For example, a team member who is a mother can stay home with a sick child and not feel the pressure she might experience at a big company."

Terri Brock, an agent in Columbia, South Carolina, says: "Balance is imperative. Naturally, I have high expectations for the agency, but I also have high expectations for my life away from work. I want to be a good wife and mother. I finally came to grips with the fact that I don't have to do everything at the agency. Time is precious, so I've become a better delegator."

A big part of working smarter is realizing that you can't really manage time; tomorrow is coming whether you manage it or not. What you can do is manage yourself. Todd Duncan says in *Time Traps*, "We cannot manage the clock; we can only manage our thoughts and actions."

Here are some tips for better self-management:

- Minimize procrastination by being more decisive.
- Beware of perfectionism by being more flexible.
- Learn to say NO without feeling guilty.
- Believe it's easier to be organized than disorganized.
- Eliminate costly time wasters such as unnecessary meetings, junk mail, senseless text messages and tweets, solicitation calls, excessive breaks and so on.
- Use professional advisers and technology.
- Make promptness a good habit.

- Become an exceptional listener.
- Master the art of delegation.
- Be more focused by using the "Master Plan Funnel Concept" (covered earlier in this chapter).

To minimize burnout, observe these "Eight Elite Enhancers Of Longer Life":

- Get the proper amount of sleep and relaxation.
- Have regular, complete and preventive medical/dental examinations.
- Eat a balanced, sensible diet and maintain the proper weight.
- Exercise aerobically, reasonably and consistently.
- Avoid all tobacco products.
- Avoid drugs and use alcohol in moderation, if at all.
- Use home smoke detectors and wear vehicle seat belts.
- Laugh often, especially at yourself.

Manage Stress By Making Time For Serenity

Stress is your body's reaction to change, challenge, coercion or lack of control. It alters your equilibrium and can cause anxiety, depression, exhaustion, illness or even death. The Latin derivation means "to be drawn tight" or, in modern terms, "to be uptight."

Serenity is a state of peacefulness designed to relieve your tension. Frankly, a stress-free life would be boring. On the other hand, a stressed-out life can lead to burnout or worse. Somewhere between boring and burnout is a balance based on managing stress by making time for serenity. To burn brightly without burning out, you should offset stress with times of tranquility in the spiritual, mental, physical and emotional sides of your life:

Spiritual—I try to make time for a daily devotional, including Bible reading, prayer and some quite time with God. I'm active in my church. I've been on several spiritual retreats. For you, spiritual stress relief might be taking a walk in nature, going on a mission trip, serving in a soup kitchen or belonging to a civic club. I've found that when you help others and trust in God, you tend to forget about your troubles while gaining necessary stress relief and divine guidance.

Mental—I work crossword puzzles every day for a few minutes. I enjoy playing Scrabble. I find quiet places to read and reflect. It's important to stimulate your mind away from the office. These mental outlets will cause your inner peace to soar and your stress to sag.

Physical—I prefer running and working out on Nautilus equipment three times per week. At home, I go to the tranquil parks around Lake Lanier. When traveling, I seek out historic battlefields, scenic parks, rustic trails, peaceful greenways and college campuses. If you dislike running, try walking, hiking, biking, swimming, rowing or some other aerobic exercise to reduce your tension. If I can exercise regularly at sixty-nine, what's stopping you?

Emotional—Because it's good to have things to look forward to, Judy and I plan some of our tranquil times well in advance—long weekend getaways, retreats, reunions and vacations. We've found if we don't plan some of our serenity, the year has a way of getting away from us and we get stressed out. We're also big believers in having positive support groups—family, friends and a small church group that meets in our homes every Wednesday evening.

To get the most out of life, make time to answer these five crucial questions:

- *Who* am I? (Principles) This is about your beliefs.
- *Why* am I here? (Purpose) This is about your reason for being.
- *Where* am I going? (Preparation) This is about goal setting.
- *How* will I get there? (Performance) This is about goal getting.
- *When* I get there, *what* will I have? (Perspective) This is about true success.

Finally, if you want to know more about work/life balance, you might want to read my book *Burn Brightly Without Burning Out.*

CALL TO ACTION

What do you need to DO after reading this chapter?

Chapter 24:

LEAVING A LEGITIMATE LEADERSHIP LEGACY

"There is no success without a successor."
–Peter Drucker

Theme:
Will you be remembered more for making money or making a difference?

Key Points:
- The pursuit of possessions is temporary
- The preeminence of people is precious
- The progression from success to significance is eternal

Earl Masters was an extraordinary leader who made a notable difference in my life as a role model and mentor. He was a master salesman who earned a good income most of his life. Yet Earl always valued people more than possessions, and significance more than success. Here's what a eulogist said at his funeral on December 6, 1993:

- Earl was true to himself (integrity).
- Earl was an encourager of others (inspiration).
- Earl was a humble servant of God (influence).
- Earl lives on after death (immortality).

The fact that you're reading about Earl Masters all these years later is an enduring tribute to a great man. **Key questions:** How will you be remembered? Will it be more for making money and success, or for making a difference and significance?

If you've done well as an agent, you might be wondering what successors have to do with success. You've made a lot of money. You've acquired a lot of nice possessions. You've traveled all over the world. You've got a big retirement account. You've even donated generously to some worthy causes over the years. Isn't that enough of a legacy?

The answer is a resounding no if you believe that your success hinges on the cultivation of successors. Tom Wright, an agent in Porterville, California, agrees. "At sixty-two, I'm at a point in my agency where I'm not doing this for the money anymore. I've found that if you just like to help people, you'll end up with money anyway. I want to leave a legacy of giving back to others. This isn't a job or even a career. This is my life's work."

The Pursuit Of Possessions Is Temporary

You've probably heard people say that "money is the root of all evil." That's untrue. You could put a million dollars in the garage of your home and if no one knew this stash was there, it would cause no harm. The correct statement is this: "For the *love* of money is at the root of all kinds of evil" (I Timothy 6:10, NLV). It's your view of money that matters.

Of course, anyone who says money isn't important is probably talking about Confederate money. Money IS important. Money buys food, clothing and shelter to sustain life. Money makes modern conveniences possible. Money offers a safety net during tough times. Money provides a security blanket for the retirement years. Money, and specifically profit, is how companies grow their businesses and hire more people. Yes, money IS important, but are you greed driven or creed oriented?

Greed-driven people always want more money so they can acquire more things. They do whatever it takes—sometimes illegally and unethically—to succeed financially. Wealth becomes an obsession, a reason for being. As long as there's more money and more things, all seems well. Yet the greed that drives such obsession is the very poison that often destroys these people. To paraphrase the famous line in the movie *Wall Street*, greed is *not* good.

Creed-oriented people appreciate the things money can buy, but they know that if they lost everything, they'd still have the core values that enabled them to earn a living in the first place. Rex Farrior, the attorney for Jack Eckerd of Eckerd Drug Stores, said in *Eckerd: Finding The Right Prescription*, "When a man has money, if you want to judge him, find out two things: how he made it, and what he does with it." Well, Mr. Eckerd earned his money honestly, and he has donated millions of dollars to charitable causes.

Money—and the convenience it buys—will never provide long-term fulfillment when greed is the driving force. The quest for true riches isn't found in the insatiable thirst for more and more possessions because enough is never enough. It's about being content with whatever you have. It's realizing that true riches are found in people, principles and purposes, not pride, possessions and petty greed.

John Templeton, a wealthy man, is known as "the dean of global investing." Moreover, hundreds of his clients have become millionaires over many decades. Yet when Mr. Templeton was asked to name the best investment he'd ever made, he probably shocked a lot of people by saying: "The most risk-free investment, the most rewarding investment, is tithing. It means giving 10 percent of your income to the church and charities. I have never known anyone who regretted this investment."

Tithing is a Biblical principle. The temptation is often to keep as much for yourself and give away as little as possible. In reality, everything you have belongs to God. You're merely the steward of the bountiful riches that are placed in your care. Stewardship is the wise management of what you've been entrusted with on this earth. A good steward is more concerned with the prudent *use* of money rather than its mere accumulation. Greed should never be a factor.

In *Money, Sex & Power*, Richard J. Foster addresses the light and dark sides of these three topics. Interestingly, money is listed first in his book title. The dark side of money is greed, the dark side of sex is lust, and the dark side of power is pride. Foster maintains: "The dark side of money inevitably leads to greed, which leads to vengeance, which leads to violence. The great moral question of our time is how to move from greed to generosity. The vow of simplicity points the way."

As an agency leader who can make a great deal of money in your career, here's your challenge: What is the wise thing to do financially and morally with your assets? **Suggestions:** Monitor your expenses. Save as much as possible. Donate as much as possible. Reinvest your profits into promoting your agency brand and hiring top talent. Do some estate planning to make sure your wealth is directed toward the right people and causes after your demise.

The Preeminence Of People Is Precious

An agent approached me and wanted to talk about the legacy part of my presentation. He said: "Dick, why should I be concerned about my legacy? I might be remembered for a couple of generations but after that, I'll be long gone and most likely forgotten. Why should I waste valuable time thinking about my legacy when it probably won't be remembered fifty or a hundred years from now?"

Unfortunately, this man didn't understand that a legacy—good or bad—is passed on from generation to generation even if specific names aren't recalled over time. Your words and ways are being watched by family, friends, neighbors, coworkers and even strangers. You don't always know how deeply you're impacting these people. If for no other reason, it behooves you to care about your legacy for the sake of all those who'll live on after you've passed away. If you've touched enough lives in a meaningful way during your career, your impact on people will be far greater than you can imagine.

David Haymon, an agent in Leesville, Louisiana, took over his father's agency after Gene retired. "Dad was a very successful agent, but he now realizes that his past achievements are no longer important. What sustains him now is the impact he made on so many people in our community. It's not about pins and plaques; it's about relationships. That's what endures. It's very satisfying to know you've helped someone save for retirement or send a kid to college."

Another agent who truly understands the importance of leaving a legitimate leadership legacy is Cliff Ourso in Donaldsonville, Louisiana. I've had the privilege of visiting Cliff's agency twice to do training for his team. You can't go anywhere in Ascension Parish without having lengthy conversations with the people Cliff has built relationships with over his impressive career. He seems to know everyone in this part of Cajun Country.

In a concise, convicting video entitled "A Legacy Of Life," Cliff talks about how his father was an insurance agent for many years in Donaldsonville before his untimely death at forty-six. Falcon Ourso had heart problems and was uninsurable. However, this didn't stop him from talking to his clients about life insurance. Cliff has delivered a lot of death claims on policies written by his father. Surviving family members are still talking about Falcon Ourso and the difference he made in their lives.

Now, the son is carrying on the tradition of his father. Cliff believes so strongly in life insurance that his goal is to have a billion dollars of it in force in his town of 7,900 people. Cliff urges other agents to learn all they can about the various life products. "It's one of the most rewarding things you can do. We have an opportunity to help a lot of people." When Cliff talks about "A Legacy Of Life," he's certainly walking his talk.

The Progression From Success To Significance Is Eternal

Making money is necessary to sustain a living. But no matter how much wealth you accumulate in a lifetime, it becomes the property of others at your death. For sure, your money won't be going with you to the grave—and would certainly be worthless if it did.

Making a difference is about your legacy. It's how you'll be remembered by others. Unlike money, a legacy—whether good or bad—is yours forever when you pass away. Typically, making money is linked to success while making a difference is associated with significance through succession.

The essence of successor leadership, significance and true success is found in multiplying your influence and thereby strengthening your legacy. Professional achievements are admirable, but they'll no longer be relevant at your death. A meaningful eulogy will be someone saying you were a loving parent, faithful spouse, loyal friend, caring mentor, dedicated servant at your place of worship, and a person who passed on the baton of leadership to many successors.

You read about my mentor Earl Masters at the beginning of this chapter. I wanted to do something special to honor his legacy, but my efforts were coming up empty. About six months after Earl's funeral, I was speaking at Amicalola Lodge in the scenic Blue Ridge Mountains of north Georgia. I had a free afternoon and decided to write a poem as a tribute to Earl. It was a gorgeous day and the words were flowing freely. Here's what I wrote:

When I've Passed Away, What Will They Say?
By Dick Biggs

Did you lend a hand to someone today?
Did you touch a heart in a special way?
Did you give your best on this blessed earth?
Did you model the truth of your human worth?

Life's so fleeting it would be such a shame,
If you failed to honor your given name.
Set your standards high for others to follow,
Lead by example, lest your words ring hollow.

You're living your legacy, what will it be?
Is your life a beacon for all to see?
Did you seize each moment with full emotion?
Did you make a difference with firm devotion?

Don't squander time, there's much you can do
In the precious days God has given you.
May these words be your motto, this I pray:
When I've passed away, what will they say?

CALL TO ACTION

What do you need to DO after reading this chapter?

Chapter 25:

CROSSING THE GREATEST GAP INLIFE ©

"The deepest knowing comes only in doing."
–Os Guinness, *Time For Truth*

Theme:
Will you go beyond knowing to doing and reach your full potential?

Key Points:
- Knowing can make you smart
- Doing can make you successful
- Bridging life's greatest gap with self-discipline

The Greatest Gap In Life © is the one between knowing and doing. You probably already know much of what you've read in these pages. However, if you aren't taking action, what's holding you back? You can only reach your full potential by implementing the ideas you're exposed to in various learning opportunities, including this book.

What I love about my career is inspiring people to take action. It's truly humbling and gratifying to know that your written or spoken words have the power to change someone's life. This is why, at sixty-nine, I haven't thought seriously about retirement other than financial preparation. I'm having too much fun helping others cross life's greatest gap. You might say my senior citizen motto is "I aspire to inspire until I expire!"

Procrastination and perfectionism are the biggest enemies of action. Procrastination is the subtle art of sabotaging your potential. The procrastinator spends a lifetime in the twilight zone between thinking and doing. The result is overanalyzing and underachieving. In short, to procrastinate is to delay starting something you know you should do.

I call it the "Procrastinator's Plight" when you say these types of things:

- I'm overwhelmed by the size of the task.
- I have too many competing priorities.
- I have a poor sense of urgency.
- I'll make too many mistakes.
- I don't have enough knowledge.
- I'm avoiding the pain of an unpleasant task.

By contrast, perfectionism is a compulsion to never finish something because you want it to be faultless. I took forever to get my first book to the publisher because it had to be perfect. In spite of my meticulousness, the first printing contained at least two errors. I quoted someone from a seminary but left off the "y" and it read "seminar"! I also quoted a United States ambassador to the United Nations, but it read "United States ambassador to the United States"!

Indeed, these were small mistakes that most people probably never caught. They were corrected on the second printing, but I learned a valuable lesson about perfectionism. Good intentions don't guarantee perfect results. Ralph Waldo Emerson was correct when he said, "Do the thing and you shall have the power."

If you say any of the following things, you might have the "Perfectionist's Plague":

- I can't let this go until the timing is just right.
- I need more time for study and analysis.
- I'm an expert, so everything I say must be acceptable to everyone.
- I must make sure my work is completely accurate.
- I must do my work more excellently than anyone.
- I'm the only one who can do this job the right away.

Knowing Can Make You Smart

We're living in the information age, so knowledge is more easily accessible than ever. Anyone who isn't informed in the twenty-first century is apathetic ("I don't need to learn"), lazy ("I don't want to learn") or a combination of both. If you have this uninspired mind-set, it will keep your agency from reaching its full potential.

I don't have a college degree. Despite being a serious student my last three years of high school, I dropped out of college three times. These weren't goals I remember setting, but it's the truth. I left the University of South Carolina after running out of money. I left Old Dominion University to go on marine embassy duty in Europe. I left Georgia State University because my work schedule as an Associated Press staff writer left little time to study. My "degree" was earned at the School of Hard Knocks—four years of service in the US Marine Corps!

Most of the people in my audiences have college degrees. If you've earned a degree(s) from an institution(s) of higher learning, you have my utmost respect. Regardless of your academic background, though, here are the crucial questions: Are you making the most of whatever education you have? Are you a lifelong learner?

Doing Can Make You Successful

I started running in 1964 to get ready for Marine Corps boot camp. With the exception of three lazy years in the early 1970s, I've been running ever since. I *know* how to stay fit and healthy, but it's the *doing* that's made it possible for nearly five decades. Knowledge isn't power; *applied* knowledge is power.

People often ask how I've stayed so steady (and injury free) with my physical fitness regimen. Well, I have a self-discipline partner. My running buddy is an annual log. I record my distances, times, locations, weather conditions and more in this little journal. My running log occupies a special place on my bedroom night stand—and I don't like to see it empty at the end of a week.

These logs date back to the late 1970s. No one else looks at them. I'm quite certain these personal records won't be of value to anyone at my death. Yet this basic self-discipline, self-accountability tool has helped keep me stay fit and healthy for a half century while crossing the gap between knowing and doing in the physical fitness area of my life.

If you struggle with self-discipline, have you considered asking for help? Do have accountability partners or mentors? Do you participate in a study club? Do you use an external coach or consultant? Do you meet regularly with a group of caring people from your place of worship? Do you keep a journal? Whatever it is, find something that works and stick with it.

You're either executing or making excuses. Which is it? Nike's "Just Do It!" was one of the most successful advertising campaigns of all time. These three simple words are the difference between a wish list and great achievements. Astute Ben Franklin said it bluntly: "He who is good at making excuses is seldom good at anything else."

Each spring when I look at a certain insurance company magazine, the front cover features the names and photos of the top ten agents from the previous year. I marvel at the steep odds of reaching this pinnacle of success because this company has thousands of agents. Clearly, every agent can't BE the best, but all agents should DO their best regardless of where they finish in the production standings. Honestly, are you doing your best to lead your agency to greatness?

Bridging Life's Greatest Gap With Self-Discipline

Discipline is "self-control" or "an orderly pattern of behavior." To cross life's greatest gap—the one between knowing and doing—many desirable qualities are required, including discipline. More specifically, self-discipline is the ability to change your bad habits into good ones.

An anonymous author offered this advice: "Take me, train me, be firm with me, and I will place the world at your feet. Be easy with me and I will destroy you. Who am I? I am habit."

In the marines, discipline is taught and modeled from boot camp until discharge/retirement. To fulfill its purpose, the corps knows its leathernecks must have an abundance of good habits or they'll be mastered by their bad habits. Accordingly, marines are held accountable for their actions. If they do well, they get promotions, pay raises, choice assignments and medals. If they behave badly, they receive demotions, fines, court martials and even imprisonment.

Obviously, you can't force your team members to be disciplined in the same way as the Marine Corps. What you can do is model good habits to your team. Are you prompt? Are you a superb listener? Are you knowledgeable? Are you a patient teacher? Do you take careful notes and follow up? Do you fulfill your promises? Essentially, are you a self-disciplined professional?

Early in my career, I discovered a pamphlet entitled *The Common Denominator Of Success,* a classic work on self-discipline and the formation of good habits. Written by the late Albert E. N. Gray, an executive with a top insurance company, this powerful message was first delivered during the 1940 convention of the National Association Of Life Underwriters (NALU) in Philadelphia, Pennsylvania. Here are four of the timeless truths from his memorable speech:

Successful people form the habit of doing things that failures don't like to do. Failures don't like organizing, prospecting, being rejected, keeping records and following up. Guess what: a lot of successful agents dislike these activities, but they understand that you have to do some things you don't like to do to get what you really want.

Successful people are more influenced by pleasing results than by pleasing methods. Making calls, setting appointments, overcoming objections and getting policies processed can be a grueling process. However, successful agents are more focused on production than on processes.

Successful people understand the difference between unconscious bad habits and conscious good habits. If you forget to set your alarm clock, it's an unconscious bad habit. It takes a conscious act or good habit to remember to set your alarm clock and show up on time at the agency. **Fact:** Bad habits will break you; good habits will make you.

Successful people surrender to a noble purpose and accept responsibility for their lives. If you're passionate about why you do what you do—and you refuse to make excuses for living a life of purpose—you'll be successful. Responsible agents take charge of their lives.

There are many ways to cross life's greatest gap. However, if I had to name just one character trait that would help you and your team cross this formidable abyss between knowing and doing, it's self-discipline. This is why I've taught *The Greatest Gap In Life* © principle for more than three decades.

My profession is real simple: I tell audiences what they already know but, hopefully, in a way that participants will be inspired to act on what they already know and haven't done. The difference between "I'm going to" and "I did" is self-discipline.

The following chart shows how to successfully bridge this gap between knowing and doing through self-discipline:

Bridging The Greatest Gap In Life! ©

Created By Dick Biggs To Help Agency Teams
Go Beyond Knowing To Doing Via Self-Discipline

SELF-DISCIPLINE...

...the ability to change bad habits into good habits

KNOWING	Inspiration/Motivation Habit	Prioritization Habit	Accountability Habit	DOING
(Smart)	(Stimulation)	(Significance)	(Submission)	(Success)

The Inspiration/Motivation Habit

This habit is about *stimulation*. As mentioned previously, inspiration is "any stimulus to creative thought" and motivation is "some inner drive, impulse or intention that causes a person to do something." In short, inspiration is about thinking; motivation is about doing. You can inspire your team members to reach their vast potential, but it's up to them to be self-motivated enough to act on your stimulation.

The Prioritization Habit

This habit is about *significance*. If something is really important, it has to be a focused priority or you'll be distracted by procrastination and perfectionism. Here's my 5Ds system for prioritization:

- **D**etermine the importance. Is it really a priority?
- **D**eadline it. When will it get done?
- **D**ecide on a plan of implementation. How will it get done?
- **D**elegate if possible. Is there someone else who can do it better?
- **D**o it. Am I executing or making excuses?

The Accountability Habit

This habit is about *submission*. The idea is to willingly surrender to accountability. To refuse to welcome accountability is to suffer the consequences of a stagnant agency and diminished legacy. Here's a summary:

- **Inspiration/Motivation** is about s*timulation,* or what drives you.
- **Prioritization** is about *significance,* or when you get things done.
- **Accountability** is about *submission,* or who holds you responsible for your actions.

If you follow this plan on your journey from smart to success, it will enable you to bridge life's greatest gap—the one between knowing and doing—with self-discipline!

Greatness is within or you wouldn't have been selected to be a leader. Don't settle for mediocrity, complacency or good enough. Instead, be an agency leader who's never haunted by the regret of unrealized dreams and who's forever comforted by your daring decision to pursue greatness.

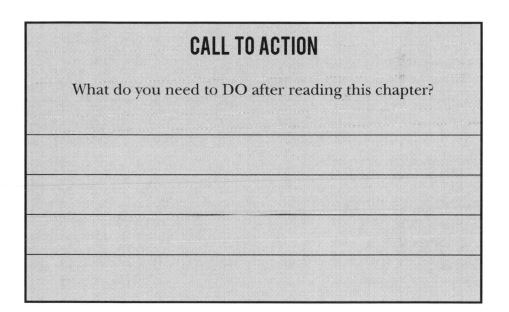

CALL TO ACTION

What do you need to DO after reading this chapter?

EPILOGUE

In my seminars, I often share some of the success strategies that have made Scott Foster a legend among his peers. It's not unusual for less accomplished agents to say things like "Scott is a machine. My agency could never be that big. I'm in a much smaller market than Scott. I don't want to work that hard." Scott has a twenty-one-team agency, but when I first spoke to his organization in 1990, he had nine employees.

Scott began his career with another insurance company in 1973 before starting a scratch agency in 1976 with the company he's represented since then. He has built an incredible small business selling the full range of insurance and financial service products. Scott has been a top-ten agent for most of his storied career. I could go on about his vast list of accomplishments, but that would take far too many pages.

Knowing and observing Scott since 1989, I believe the one thing that separates him from many other agents is the size of his thinking! Early in his career, at the urging of his field leader, Scott bought a two-story office building and rented it out for years to pay the mortgage and generate extra revenue. This magnificent edifice is now occupied solely by Scott's team. Scott knew he could grow a bigger team if he sold a lot of higher commission life insurance. And Scott realized he could produce a lot more capital for growth if he maximized his annual bonus.

If you're coasting or complacent, what's keeping you from being a fully engaged agent? You have a good education. You can learn to be a better leader. You can increase the quantity of your self-motivation by raising the quality of your inspiration. You can work harder without working all the time. You certainly control your attitude.

Agency growth is linked closely to the size of your thinking. Don't be sabotaged by complacency. Don't be paralyzed by the fear of change. Don't be unwilling to take some risks. Don't have frequent gripe sessions with negative agents. These are unproductive habits associated with status quo agents.

If you're serious about agency growth, here are some of the success strategies that Scott Foster shared with me a few years ago:

Surround yourself with good people. Your agency success is dependent upon the people you choose as your business partners. Scott has several team members who've been with him for ten to twenty years or more. He goes beyond gaining good people to training, sustaining and retaining his peak-performing team. High turnover is a costly expense, but investing in productive, loyal people is the best investment you'll ever make.

Work hard. Taking time off is important, but there's no substitute for working hard and leading by example at your agency. Scott does an admirable job of balancing the demands of professional success with the benefits of personal happiness.

Love what you do. Here's what actress Betty White said upon turning ninety: "Why should I retire when people keep asking me to do something I love to do?" If you truly love your profession, you'll be an involved leader. Scott could retire at any time, but he loves what he does.

Have the full support of your spouse. You'll obviously have a different support system if you're single. But as any happily married agent knows, success at work won't translate to happiness at home if both spouses aren't on the same page concerning the level of agency commitment. Linda, Scott's wife, works part-time at the agency, but they're also very deliberate about enjoying life outside of the office.

Maintain a high level of integrity. Scott's impeccable reputation is the foundation of every interaction he has with his team members, customers and everyone else. When you're dealing with a customer's money, risks and dreams, trust isn't optional. As you know well, the quickest way to lose your agency is to do something unethical or illegal.

Beware of micromanaging. Scott used to lead his annual agency planning retreat until his team said his meetings were boring. Being a wise leader, Scott accepted this feedback and asked his four team leaders to plan the next retreat. It was a big success. **Lesson learned:** Let go and watch the team grow.

Grow multiline. This will increase customer loyalty and boost your bottom line significantly. If this is a weak area for you, seek the advice of agents who are successful in multi-lining. Scott's suggestion: "Devote at least 30 percent of your time on life insurance sales."

Do periodic customer reviews. Scott has mastered this activity. He believes the ideal time to offer this service is between eighteen and thirty-six months. On a good day, Scott will do six of them.

Monitor your goals. Clearly, Scott is a big goal-setter based on his remarkable track record. But to be a great goal-getter, you have to review your goals regularly and be willing to hold team members accountable for their stated intentions. It's always shocking to hear how many agents don't make this a mandatory team requirement.

No agent starts on top. Long-term success comes from casting a vision of where you want the agency to go and then chipping away daily at the annual goals regardless of any circumstances, challenges and changes that are encountered. Henry Ford shared this wisdom more than a century ago: "Think you can, think you can't, either way, you'll be right!"

Remember, the only one who controls the size of your thinking is you. Scott and I implore you to take a leap of faith and THINK BIG. You will, won't you?

ACTION PLAN

"What I most need is someone or something to get me
to do what I already know how to do and what I've already
said I wanted to do."
–Ralph Waldo Emerson

What will you do differently after reading this book? You certainly
can't do everything at once, but you can do something—starting
right now with an action plan. Because less is often more, please
list your top three action ideas and deadlines for completion in
the spaces provided:

Idea	Deadline	Done	Impact
————	———	———	———
————	———	———	———
————	———	———	———
————	———	———	———
————	———	———	———
————	———	———	———
————	———	———	———
————	———	———	———
————	———	———	———
————	———	———	———

After you've implemented each idea, check it off in the "done"
area and summarize the impact of your results. Then, review your
"call to action" notes at the end of each chapter and decide on additional ways to improve.

Knowing is important. Understanding is imperative. But wisdom requires implementation of what you know and understand. Do so and your journey to greatness will be merry, meaningful and memorable.

RECOMMENDED LEADERSHIP BOOKS

- *Courage To Lead*—Charlie Farrell
- *Developing The Leader Within You*—John Maxwell
- *Developing The Leaders Around You*—John Maxwell
- *Leadership Is An Art*—Max De Pree
- *Leaders Ought To Know*—Phillip Van Hooser
- *Making A Difference: Twelve Qualities That Make You A Leader*—Sheila Murray Bethel
- *On Becoming A Leader*—Warren Bennis
- *Principle-Centered Leadership*—Stephen R. Covey
- *Quiet Leadership*—David Rock
- *Robert E. Lee On Leadership*—Wess Roberts
- *The Effective Executive*—Peter Drucker
- *The Leadership Challenge*—James M. Kouzes & Barry Z. Posner
- *The Leadership Lessons Of Jesus*—Bob Briner & Ray Pritchard
- *The Moral Leader*—Sandra J. Sucher
- *The 21 Indispensable Qualities Of A Leader*—John Maxwell
- *The 21 Irrefutable Laws Of Leadership*—John Maxwell
- *The Top Ten Mistakes Leaders Make*—Hans Finzel
- *Visioneering*—Andy Stanley
- *Wooden On Leadership*—Coach John Wooden
- *You Don't Need A Title To Be A Leader*—Mark Sanborn

SCOTT FOSTER BIO

Scott Foster is an icon within the company he's represented since 1976. Since starting a scratch agency in Conyers, Georgia, Scott has grown it to more than six thousand households by offering a full range of insurance products and financial services. His agency is represented by a team of twenty-one peak-performing professionals.

Scott was a National Honor Society qualifier and finished in the top ten students in a class of 605 at Jordan Vocational High School in Columbus, Georgia. He graduated magna cum laude from the University of Georgia with a degree in risk management and insurance. Scott earned his CLU designation and is a life and qualifying member of the Million Dollar Round Table.

Scott has been a top-ten agent sixteen times—a remarkable feat in a company represented by thousands of agents. In addition, he has led this company twenty-one times as the number one life insurance agent and has never finished out of the top ten.

Scott was involved in the second phase of a comprehensive agent development program to help his peers reach their full potential. He has spoken more than two hundred times within his profession, including three times at MDRT annual conventions and multiple times at CLU events.

Active in his community, Scott has chaired many committees and served as president of his Kiwanis and Rotary clubs. He has been a Sunday school teacher at his church for twenty-five years. He's also a member of the Eastminster School Board of Directors.

Scott has run thirty-five half marathons and fifteen marathons, including the 2008 Boston Marathon. He also enjoys reading great books and sending them to his many friends.

Married for forty-one years and counting, he and his wife, Linda, have two grown daughters, Susan and Laura, and two grandchildren. Scott's brother Marvin is a retired insurance agent and his son-in-law Jason Collins is a successful agent in Warner Robins, Georgia.

Scott's agency is located at 1080 Iris Drive, Conyers, Georgia 30094, 770-483-0632. His email is scott@scottfosteragency.com.

DICK BIGGS BIO

Known as "the a-line-ment specialist," Dick works with organizations to boost *bottom line* profits and better the *top line*—people and their productivity. He does this as a keynote speaker, seminar leader and author. His topics are leadership, mentoring, communication, teamwork and work/life balance.

Dick has traveled to all fifty states and several foreign nations to serve a diverse group of clients—Fortune 500 companies, small businesses, government agencies, trade associations, educational institutions and nonprofits.

He's the author of *Burn Brightly Without Burning Out, If Life Is A Balancing Act, Why Am I So Darn Clumsy?* and *Wisdom Gold*. He's also the creator of "Maximize Your Moments With The Masters," a comprehensive mentoring program licensed to a variety of organizations.

Prior to starting his business in 1982, Dick was a sportswriter for the *Atlanta Constitution* and staff writer for the Associated Press. He also spent thirteen years in sales/sales management and graduated at the top of his Sales Training, Inc. (STI) class.

A marine sergeant, Dick served as a security guard at the American embassies in Warsaw, Poland, and Rome, Italy. After completing seven marathons, thirteen half marathons and thirty Peachtree Road Races in his prime years, Dick now runs fifteen or so miles every week and is a co-founder of the Chattahoochee Road Runners—the second-largest running club in Georgia.

In addition, Dick is a past president of the National Speakers Association–Georgia and a recipient of the Kay Herman Legacy Award, this chapter's highest honor.

Dick is married to Judy and they reside on Lake Lanier north of Atlanta. They have two grown daughters, Rebecca and Tara, a son-in-law, Bo, and a thirteen-year-old grandson, Jackson. Dick and Judy are small group leaders at their church. Dick mentored Scotty Cole from the first grade through his high school graduation in 2012. Dick loves solving crossword puzzles, reading, traveling and rooting for the Georgia Bulldogs.

Dick is president of Biggs Optimal Living Dynamics (BOLD!), 9615 Settlers Lane, Gainesville, GA 30506. Contact him at 770-886-3035 or biggspeaks@mindspring.com. His website is www.biggspeaks.com.

Made in the USA
Columbia, SC
06 March 2019